PRAISE FOR A WAY OUT

"Michelle takes you on a journey of highs and lows as she deals with depression, social anxiety, and suicidal thoughts. Her struggles pave a path for anyone struggling to see hope and to realize, as she says, "You can do this." Michelle reveals in detail her continual battle with depression and its effect on friends and family. A must-read for anyone struggling or wanting to know more about mental illness."

—KEVIN R. BRIGGS, Sergeant, California Highway Patrol (Ret.), author of *Guardian of the Golden Gate: Protecting the Line Between Hope and Despair*

"I recommend this honest, uplifting, heartbreaking, and hilarious book to anyone who is struggling, anyone who has overcome challenges, and anyone who wants to better understand a compassionate approach to mental illness and raise their own awareness of mental health—so I recommend this book to all of us."

—REBECCA GIBSON, founder of Orange Daisy Project (supporting teen girls' mental health)

"Michelle Balge cares about her readers, and shares her darkest moments in the hopes that others will feel validated and understood. Her journey, though a difficult one, is troublingly common as depression and anxiety are on the rise, but it's inspiring to know she found her way back to a good life."

—JESSICA HOLMES, comedian, author of *I Love Your Laugh* and *Depression The Comedy*

"A Way Out is an honest, compassionate, and informative story of one young woman's struggle with severe depression and social anxiety. The writer reveals a candid and honest recollection of her experience with mental illness. This courageous mental health advocate has written a powerful memoir that empowers its readers, making them feel they are not alone in their struggles."

—NUMILA PARKER, MSW, Parents For Children's Mental Health

"As a fellow sufferer of mental illness, I related to so many parts of Michelle's story. Her suffering was deeply felt as was her perseverance to get well and conquer her illness. Great insight on how this affects family members and loved ones. Anybody that does not understand mental illness should read this book as it gives a clear understanding of how painful and debilitating it is."

—CLINT MALARCHUK, former NHL goaltender, author of *The Crazy Game: How I Survived in the Crease and Beyond*

A

WAY

OUT

A WAY OUT

A Memoir of Conquering
Depression and Social Anxiety

MICHELLE BALGE

I have tried to recreate events, locales, and conversations to the best of my ability from my memories. In order to maintain their anonymity, in some instances I have changed the names of individuals. I haven't changed any identifying characteristics or details, such as my dad being bald. Sorry, Dad.

Visit www.michellebalge.com.

ISBN-13: 978-1-7750942-2-7 (ebook)
ISBN-13: 978-1-7750942-1-0 (paperback)
ISBN-13: 978-1-7750942-0-3 (hardcover)

Editing: Cassandra Filice/Write to the End
Cover Design: Jennifer Zemanek/Seedlings Design Studio
Flower Image: Ajgul/Shutterstock.com
Interior Design: Michelle Balge
Author Photo: Nicole Balge

First Edition: February 2018
10 9 8 7 6 5 4 3 2 1

For my loved ones; you are always there for me.
For those in dark places; you can make it through.

"I now see how owning our story and loving ourselves through that process is the bravest thing that we will ever do."

—Brené Brown, *The Gifts of Imperfection*

CONTENT WARNING

Some of what I'm sharing with you I have never told anyone. Though I have spoken at various events, there are several things I keep out—not only for myself but also to avoid the possibility of triggering anyone. Here though, I don't want to hide. You're going into this knowing that my mind has been to dark places, and I intend to share them honestly. If you feel you aren't in the right state of mind, put the book down for now. If you experience any suicidal thoughts, please call your emergency number or a helpline. Tell someone. I promise you that there are people who care.

CONTENTS

PREFACE

SINCE THE BEGINNING of my recovery, I've tinkered with the idea of writing a book about my experience with mental health and illness. It feels wonderful sharing my story through speeches and I believe that a memoir is another great medium to get the word out to people. This book will allow you to see much further into my thoughts than hearing me speak. Not only because speeches are shortened and I avoid any triggering content, but also because it's difficult for me to even imagine thinking the way I used to.

While writing, I had to listen to specific songs from times I was depressed to be able to bring back the negative thoughts that were once commonplace. Conversely, I listened to certain uplifting songs to write inspirational parts of this memoir.

A Way Out features my raw, unfiltered thoughts. I decided that if I'm going to share what I went through in regard to mental illness, I'm sharing it all. Why put so much effort into creating something if you're going to hide parts of yourself? I made it clear to my editor, Cassandra, that I was going to write honestly about my suicidal thoughts and not hold anything back. I needed her to be on the same page, as this was something I was not willing to sacrifice. No one was going to be changing or getting rid of my thoughts. They may be negative and make people uncomfortable or emotional, but they happened. And to me, it's important to show what I truly experienced. Thankfully, Cassandra saw things the same way I did, recognizing the value in sharing my true feelings.

This memoir is about more than just my thoughts. It's about the hardship of living with mental illness, the road to recovery, and the spaces in-between. I aspire to make a difference through my words. I'm telling my story in the hope that those experiencing mental illness can relate, those who know someone with a mental illness can better understand, and those just interested in the topic can learn more. I want to break the stigma. If only one person benefits, it will all be worth it.

Our society has come a long way in recent years recognizing mental illnesses for what they are: illnesses just like a physical illness, but of the mind. We're beginning to see mental health being promoted as something just as important to maintain as physical health. Campuses such as Brock University are now incorporating Wellness Weeks (called by other names elsewhere) to teach students the importance of self-care, to normalize talking openly about mental health, and to broaden awareness of the resources available.

We're even going beyond trying to normalize conversations about mental health by altering the words we use. It's no longer socially acceptable to say someone committed suicide, as they didn't commit any crime. They died by suicide or lost their life to suicide.

I'm not going to say that everything is hunky-dory and we've reached the point where the world of mental health acceptance is filled with sunshine and rainbows. There are many obstacles we're still facing, such as a lack of access to resources, lack of education, and discrimination. It's still difficult for people to reach out for help because of the stigma surrounding mental illness.

Now, I'm not saying I'm going to singlehandedly change anything, but perhaps the insights into my mind and illnesses can educate others in a way that helps them to see what happens when depression takes over. When social anxiety takes over. When the negative thoughts in your head go from troublesome to grueling. When you're teetering on the fence between life and death. It's not selfish. It's really not. Yes, you're consumed by self-hate when on that fence, but it's because you believe others are better off without you here. The world needs to see this side of things. Perhaps you've read about it before or experienced it for yourself. Either way, it's important to get the message out that mental illnesses are serious and they're real. We can all take actions to improve the way society views mental health and illness, as well as adjust our own perceptions.

In the summer of 2016, I wrote a poem about my experience with depression and the negative thoughts I had from social anxiety. I called it "A Way Out." Less than a year later, in the spring of 2017, it hit me that I was ready and committed to writing a book. Baring all my thoughts for the world to see. Within a week I had written almost half of my first draft, titling it after the poem. When I'm passionate about a topic or project I'm working on, I go all out. This is my all out: showing my way out.

A Way Out

I'm consumed by darkness,
there is no way out.

No way out of my mind that traps me.
No way out of this despair that overwhelms me.
No way out of this life.
What can I do when the tears run out?
When the only solace is hoping I will fall asleep and not wake up.
But I will wake up.
Not from choice, but from life.
The life I don't want.
The life I don't deserve.
The life where nothing is wrong but me.
Where I pray to someone I don't believe in,
just in hopes this will end.
But it doesn't.

Day by day, night by night,
I get through it.
It is difficult, the hardest thing I have ever done,
but I get through it.
If those who say they love me actually do, can I do this to them?
Can I risk hurting those I love?
I push the feelings of wanting to end away,
even if it's till the next morning or in a few days.
The feelings won't last, they are not forever.
What is forever is what means most. Family, friends, love.
I will fight my way out of this pit,
this pit that sucks me in every chance it gets.

I will find and develop the right tools to help me,
that will help to pull me out.
The journey will be difficult, impossible maybe.

But I did it.
I went through the journey and survived.
I crawled out of the muddy pit of my seemingly worth-
less existence.
I now see value in my life.
I see more light in this world, in me.
The darkness that literally and figuratively consumed
me is gone.
Don't give up.
Please don't give up.
There are people who love you, people who care.
Some day one of those people will be you.

PROLOGUE

I HIDE EVERYTHING. I hide my pain, hide my feelings, and hide myself from others. I'm trapped in my mind. I sit in the darkness of my room and stare at the wall for hours, thoughts of suicide circling in my head. Then I cry uncontrollably until there are no more tears. I go to bed early because sleep is one of the only parts of life I can enjoy. The part where maybe it can take me away from everything for good. But I always wake up.

I go to high school in a daze and just happen to always be tired if my friends ask what's wrong. It isn't a total lie,

I am always tired, but it's more than that. It is hopeless-ness, it is guilt, it is shame, sadness, anger, despair, and being overwhelmed all at once. There are too many feel-ings to explain, yet I also feel nothing. I am nothing. I am worthless and have no point in living. Nearly every day I tell myself that I'm nothing and look in the mirror to tell myself I look disgusting.

"I am nothing. I am disgusting." Why would anyone care if I were gone? Wouldn't it be better that way? I want to disappear, for good. I want to die. The urges are so strong I collapse and cry, but tell myself to wait till morn-ing. The impulses are so forceful I lie down shaking and sobbing, my hands underneath my back so as not to reach for the pills. How did I get here?

A
WAY
OUT

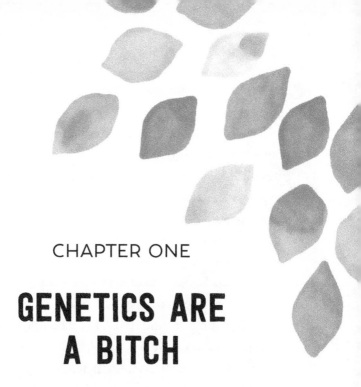

CHAPTER ONE

GENETICS ARE A BITCH

MY GREAT-GRANDFATHER on my mom's side of the family, who died before I was born, experienced psychosis. I've only ever heard two stories about him. One is that he would chase his daughter, my grandmother, around the kitchen table with a knife. Another is he would throw bales of hay down to his pregnant wife and laugh as she caught them, with my grandma watching. I don't think anyone can imagine what it would feel like to have to go through those experiences as a child, let alone from your own father, but my grandma was, and is, very strong.

In her adult life she experienced depression at different points in time, contemplating suicide, and most recently endured depression's hard falls when my grandpa passed away. She had lost her partner, her rock, and fell into a deep depression that landed her in the hospital.

My mom received a call from my grandma's doctor who was seriously concerned for Grandma's wellbeing, and he asked Mom to take her to the hospital. Mom and Dad drove to my grandma's house right away and were surprised by what she did next. Grandma told them where her will was, asked what jewelry of hers Mom wanted, and tried to give them cash. My parents immediately took her to the hospital, thankfully willingly, and she remained there for five days until she was no longer suicidal. She then saw a psychiatrist who put her on medication for the first time and her outlook on life has now completely turned around.

My mom experienced depression and anxiety as an adult, never telling my sisters or me about this until we ourselves experienced it. Mom thought it was normal to feel depressed because that was how her mom always was, so she never did anything about it. She also had anxiety driving, afraid of driving over bridges and stopping at busy intersections for fear of passing out: it was like waiting at the top of a rollercoaster, trying to prepare for the fall, but in her case, a panic attack. She eventually stopped driving to work, preferring the bus, and then became too fearful to drive at all. This spurred her to see a doctor, going on medication that helped both her anxiety and depression.

My older sister, Lindsay, experienced anxiety, while my younger sister, Nicole, experienced depression. Lindsay first had anxiety when working as a registered nurse and it became more burdensome as she began studying for her master's degree while working full-time. She went on a medication to aid her and has been doing well since.

Nicole became depressed when she was thirteen and never allowed herself to let her emotions out through talking to someone or even crying. This prompted her to self-harm, by cutting, as a way to let out these emotions. Though for a short time it helped her to put her hurt somewhere else, the cutting left her feeling more depressed in the end. Mom spent months sleeping in Nicole's room with her, to show her support and make sure Nicole didn't hurt herself. Nicole also went on medication, though finding the right fit and combination proved difficult.

There was a point in time when Nicole and I were both depressed, wanting to kill ourselves, but we were determined to not let the other do so. Though my life meant nothing to me, hers sure did, and vice versa. Neither of us can remember how we encouraged each other, but we did. And it worked, along with many other sources of help.

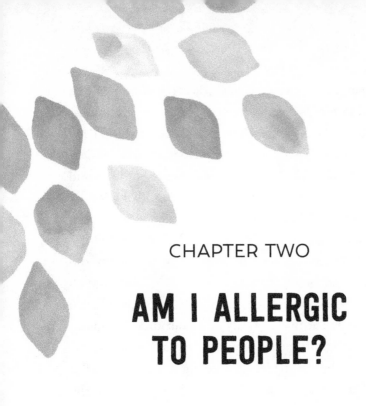

CHAPTER TWO

AM I ALLERGIC TO PEOPLE?

I HAD WHAT I think was the ideal childhood growing up in Ontario, Canada. My parents, married for over thirty-eight years now, as well as my two sisters and I, were all very close. We went on family road trips together to Florida and Eastern Canada, found fun things to do together during March break, and enjoyed going to the Canadian National Exhibition (CNE) in Toronto every summer.

My dad and I burn easily, so at the CNE—and on any outdoor adventure—we'd slather ourselves in sunscreen, he ensuring his bald head was covered with lotion or a hat. In the midst of the fun rides we would all take a break to visit and pet piglets at the "farm," trying not to breathe in the smells of manure and hay from the animals. We also went to the retail outlets at the CNE, my mom and sisters loving to shop for clothes, books, anything really.

In the winter we would go tobogganing, and drive around to find the houses with the most extravagant Christmas lights. I always looked forward to Christmas-time. Everything about it was filled with warmth, love and family. We decorated our tree with years' worth of ornaments and bright lights, the scent of pine filling the room and the needles falling down only to stick to the soles of my feet as I danced to Christmas music.

All my childhood family memories are happy memories. Actually, scratch that. During a Florida vacation when I was four I almost drowned. While floating in a swim ring with my arms and head above the cool water, a woman doing laps in the pool swam past me, creating waves. I was flipped upside down, my skinny body sliding out of the ring and to the bottom of the pool. Dad was blissfully reading his newspaper, and Mom was tanning, so it was Lindsay who noticed she couldn't see me any-more. At nine years old she dove into the water and towed me to safety. So, besides my brush with death, my child-hood family memories were quite positive.

If anything was ever bothering me I knew my parents would be there to help me. We never lied to each other, other than about Santa Claus; and I didn't figure that one out until I was ten because I trusted my parents that he was real. (My dad's story about Santa's elves working in China to explain why so many toys said 'Made in China' could only fool me for so long!) My parents rarely fought; one of the worst arguments I can remember was when Dad accidentally took Mom's car keys, and he later came home with a bouquet of flowers to apologize.

My parents chose to have three kids spaced far apart. My older sister, Lindsay, is five years older than me while my younger sister, Nicole, is seven years younger than me. My sisters and I argued a lot when we were younger, but that's typical of siblings. We still always had each other's back. As we grew older we also grew closer.

We had pets, including a bird, hamsters, cats, and currently a dog. (Not all at the same time.) These animals were a comfort to me, being easy to talk to and making me laugh. I especially bonded with our cats and dog, feeling a connection with them that I couldn't explain.

One of my two best friends, Joseph, lived right across the street from me and we spent almost all of our time together. We met when I was five and he was four, the two of us clicking instantly. Hours were spent on the phone and even more time in his pool. I'd walk around the pool with my stomach puffed out after eating, showing off how pregnant I could look in contrast to my normally skinny body. I was typically shy around people so it was nice to be able to feel comfortable around him.

You may be wondering, what does this middle class, straight, white girl in an intact nuclear family have to complain about? The truth is, I don't have anything to complain about. There were no traumatic experiences or feelings of things not being good enough. Besides genetics, however, there were embarrassing, awkward, and scary situations that could have led to increased social anxiety and the beginnings of my negative thought process.

—ℓℓ—

As I got older, I realized more and more my shyness was frequently bothering me. I would feel lonely at recess if Joseph or my other best friend, Amanda, wasn't there, because I had difficulty connecting with anyone else. Once at school I was chosen to be part of an academic competition, but was too afraid to ever hit the buzzer, even though I knew most of the answers. I should've had the guts to push it but I didn't. I had failed.

I remember looking in the mirror, perhaps at the age of eight, and wondering if I were allergic to people. Maybe it would be a good thing, because then I would have a valid excuse for not wanting to be around others. While alone, with family, or a best friend, I could dance all over the place and just be myself. It was frustrating that I was a different person around other people. They didn't get to see my humour, my outgoing side, my true personality.

I would dread going to family gatherings, afraid of having to talk to extended family members that I only saw a few times a year. I always needed a safety person with me, someone I could feel comfortable around. This meant either someone in my immediate family or a best friend.

One of the other reasons I feel uncomfortable going to these gatherings is because of a blow up I had during a Thanksgiving dinner. Well, a blow up I had, from the back end.

Filled up on milk, butter, and other dairy products, I was laughing while sitting at the kitchen table with my cousins (or as we called it, the "kid's" table) while the adults were in the dining room—and let out a huge fart. At the time I didn't know I was lactose intolerant. In fact, I wouldn't find out until right before high school. Everyone in the kitchen and dining room began laughing uproariously, my cousins pointing at me so the adults knew who dealt it. I felt so embarrassed that I just wanted to melt into the ground.

Today, no matter where I am, sitting at a kitchen table away from the majority of the adults makes me extremely uncomfortable. I always opt to either sit at the dining room table or eat wherever we'd like such as couches, but not the dreaded kitchen table. I am terrified of having that same thing repeat itself, even though it happened almost twenty years ago.

—ee

My first experience with a therapist was at nine years old, but it wasn't for depression or social anxiety. I had developed a tic in which my head would jerk forward as if in a quick nod. I would try to suppress the urge to perform this movement, but the discomfort would grow too strong and I'd have to take action. I needed to do this all the time: at home, at school, even in the bathroom. No matter where I went I couldn't control my head jerking and it was bothersome. Did other people notice? I wanted to stop, but I didn't know how.

My parents suggested I see a therapist, but I didn't see how they could talk the tic out of me. I might as well try though, I hated having this and didn't want to live the rest of my life doing something that brought attention to me.

Seeing the therapist was less intimidating than I expected. Although there was a lot of talking involved, it was more than that. She suggested things to do that could help suppress the urge to jerk my head and take my mind off of it. One of these was using a Koosh Ball with rubber strings that would keep my hands and mind busy. Another was rubbing smooth stones, one of which my therapist gave to me.

After using these tools regularly, my parents noticed that while watching TV I was no longer jerking my head. Eventually, my tic disappeared. I would still have the occasional urge to make the movement, but I turned back to the ball and stones, knowing they could help me.

It was such a relief to go to school and stand for the national anthem, not having to worry about who would see my head tic while I was supposed to be standing still. Because now, I was standing still. Although this was something I no longer had to worry about causing embarrassment, there were still plenty of other embarrassing moments for me yet to come.

—ℓℓ—

I never looked forward to giving a speech each year of grade school. In third grade, when I was eight years old, I was one of the students that had my speech completely memorized, so I only had a couple of points on my cue cards to keep me on track. (This was unlike a story my dad told me of a friend whose whole speech was "silence is golden" and he stood there for three minutes without saying a word.)

I was nervous, but I did a great job and had made it to the top two finalists. When it was time to present again, this time to determine the winner, I froze. In the middle of my speech, I forgot the words and was silent for half a minute. They used a timer and unlike my dad's friend, this wasn't planned, and it certainly wasn't golden. I looked down to my cue cards, and regretted not having everything written on them. I kept staring at the cards, willing the words to show up. Eventually I remembered, but there was no confidence in my voice for the rest of the speech. I was told I didn't win because of that pause.

Every year, for the next five years of school speeches, I was haunted by this moment. Even now when I have to give a speech or presentation I am reminded of this time.

When I was ten, my family and I moved to a small town. They told me it was because the city was too crowded, but they left out another important reason: There was a man living four doors down from us who attempted to rape an eight-year-old girl from my school. A letter was sent out to each student to make us aware, and of course I showed it to my parents, but I myself didn't fully grasp the situation.

I was dead set against moving at first because I didn't want to leave the few friends I had, but eventually I gave in. I stopped talking to Amanda, one of my two best friends, right after moving and this caused immense guilt as well as made me feel as if I failed at being a friend. I met a couple of people in my new town, Candace and Alex, and I wasn't expecting that to happen so easily.

That year, in fifth grade, Candace and I were at the mall for lunch and about to walk into Walmart. Suddenly, except for the sound of receipts being printed off, it was completely silent and everyone was standing still. We were so confused and didn't know what to think. Was someone about to win the lottery and they were all waiting to hear if the person had won? I'm not sure why that was the first thought to pop into my head, but I had no other explanation. Candace and I began giggling because of the silence and I didn't know how else to respond. It was weird seeing everyone so still and quiet.

We then heard an announcement over the loudspeaker saying they would have a moment of silence. We were unsure for what, and our giggling grew louder until we were both laughing quite vehemently, unable to stop. Our laughter echoed throughout the mall.

When there is too much silence with other people around, I begin to chuckle, like when I'm at a sleepover and it's time to finally fall asleep. But this was no sleepover. This was a serious moment and we were embarrassing ourselves. As much as I wanted to stop laughing I couldn't. Everyone was staring at us, and I mean everyone. With disapproving faces. When we got back to school we noticed our teacher had found out somehow, and gave us an even worse glare.

We later discovered that the moment of silence was for the 9/11 attacks that had just happened that day. It's not something I'm proud of. Whenever anyone talks about where they were on that day, I will never forget what I was doing, and the guilt will never leave me—forming an awful feeling in the pit of my stomach.

The reason I'm sharing this shameful story is because part of the reason why the laughing occurred was my social anxiety. There were some—well, many, truth be told—social situations when I didn't know how to respond appropriately. When my body wouldn't allow me to stop doing something I didn't want it to. In addition to this, as you know laughter can be contagious, and Candace and I fed off each other. It makes me wonder if the disapproval I faced and the subsequent guilt that I felt contributed to my negative self-talk.

Another moment I'm not proud of during fifth grade was when my other friend, Alex, had a mild allergic reaction to a plant outside during recess and needed calamine lotion on the lower half of her face. When I saw her back in class I made a joke, saying, "Well, now we all know Santa Claus exists." I don't remember if anyone laughed or not. All I saw was a look of horror and sorrow on my friend's face. I had no idea my joke would be so hurtful to her, as what I meant was that it looked as if she had a white beard.

Alex told me later that she thought I called her Santa because she was overweight. That thought never crossed my mind until she said it and I felt terrible, ashamed of myself and full of guilt. She wouldn't talk to me for two weeks, and even after that, we were never friends again. This lesson taught me not to make jokes anymore or speak in class because I would just hurt those that I cared about. If I stayed quiet, my words couldn't hurt anyone.

During recess one day, a crowd of people came up to me asking if I would date one of the boys in my class. I didn't know how to respond, and I remembered from my old school that there would be "opposite days" sometimes. If I said no, I didn't want to, would that in actuality mean yes? Or was this a normal day and no meant no? I became so flustered that I burst into tears and was brought inside by a teacher.

No one understood my reaction, and I couldn't really understand it either. There were just too many people around, looking at me, and I didn't know the right answer to give. This made me think that if anyone ever asked me out in the future, it may just be a game and it was something I had to avoid.

The next year in sixth grade, I made a new best friend, Melissa. Though we were both shy, it suited us well. We spent as much time as we could with each other at school and she was one of the few people I would see outside of classes. When we got together we weren't shy. We'd be our weird selves, laughing hysterically at each other and sometimes at nothing. I remember standing with her and a couple of others at recess pretending we were sunflowers, soaking up the sun.

The two of us talked about everything and we shared our darkest secrets, never feeling judged. She's stuck with me through thick and thin, even through a period when we didn't talk for a year because I was having too much trouble with my social anxiety and depression. I essentially only talked to family, but she was there when I was ready.

In the same year that I met Melissa, I had another extremely embarrassing moment. Our class was in a portable and I sat beside two hilarious guys. One day they had me laughing so hard that I let out a fart. I blamed it on my chair, trying to recreate the noise with it but failing. They didn't buy it because they could smell it, and a couple of other people around me heard too. I was so embarrassed but managed to pull myself together.

About a half hour later they had me laughing again and I was still feeling gassy. Mind you, the night before I ate chili for dinner, then had it as leftovers with a large glass of milk for breakfast because it was so good. I didn't know about the connection between beans and flatulence. And I still didn't know that I had a lactose intolerance. My classmates had me laughing so much I could no longer hold in what was bound to escape.

One minute we were laughing our heads off, the next I farted. Not like before, though. This was explosive. I could swear the portable shook. No lie. After my mishap there was complete silence in the room, all heads turned in my direction, jaws and eyes wide open, and then came the laughter. I know my face was bright red as I sunk into my chair.

I was about to try and make a joke out of it so I wouldn't feel so humiliated, but someone else got to it first. I am forever grateful for the one boy I was sitting beside. He took the blame, turning it into a joke by saying, "You think that's bad, I can make atomic bombs!"

I don't know how many people believed him or not, but it gave me the confidence to stay in that school. I don't think I ever even said this to him because I was so embarrassed, but thank you.

In seventh grade when I was twelve, I was told by my teacher that I had received the highest mark in the class on a geography test. I was pleasantly surprised as I was positive that I failed it since I didn't study and barely knew any of the answers. This was very unlike me, but I didn't care for the class.

When the tests were finally handed out, I didn't get mine. I was called to the teacher's desk, along with a few other students, so he could hand ours back separately. It turns out that we had received the worst marks in the class.

This incident caused me to have difficulty trusting people when they told me good things, believing that they were making it up. I still don't know if the teacher lied to me or made a mistake in telling me I had the best mark, but either way it hurt my confidence in myself and in others.

Beyond the typical school day, there were events such as school dances that we could attend. I went to one of these and chose to stay seated the whole time. I was uncomfortable dancing with friends to music and I avoided dancing with any boys because I didn't want them to think I liked them. I felt like I was the weird, quiet girl, which I quite honestly was, and assumed that no one would want to dance with me anyway. One of the guys did ask me to dance though, and he was the most popular guy in school. It was a pity dance. I didn't decline him, but I still knew it was out of sympathy. I genuinely just didn't want to dance with anyone.

That kind of social situation made me uncomfortable and I'm not sure why I went in the first place. I kept this mindset in high school and never attended any "cool" parties, only going to gatherings of close friends.

Although many of my embarrassing and stressful moments were at school, there was one particular event that occurred at home, and it's seared into my memory. I was with Lindsay in our family room when she could have died—okay, so this is definitely another bad childhood memory, with my sister almost dying instead of me.

Lindsay has a severe nut allergy so we never kept them in the house and always read the ingredients on everything we bought. While home alone with her one day she asked me to come over to her.

"Can you read the ingredients?" she asked, looking concerned.

I agreed to do so and was shocked at what I saw. Peanut paste. One of the last ingredients on the frozen dinner, but there it was. Of all the nuts, Lindsay is most allergic to peanuts. We both looked at each other with wide eyes, knowing the same thing: we had to get her to the hospital.

My first thought was to call 911 and I told her this, but she got me to call Dad, who was working an hour away—not the best first choice. Then I called Mom who worked at the hospital nearby, but her coworkers answered instead. I couldn't get my words out properly because I was crying so much. I handed the phone to Lindsay, whose mouth and throat were swelling up. Mom's coworkers were going to come and get her.

"Shouldn't we call an ambulance instead?" I asked her again, but she didn't want that.

We went downstairs to wait for our mom's coworkers to arrive and I convinced Lindsay she had to take her EpiPen. This was an emergency and if she wasn't going to accept an ambulance, she damn well was going to use her EpiPen. I went outside to let her do her thing in the house, and saw the car pull up minutes later. That EpiPen saved her life, keeping her breathing until she made it to the hospital. Dad got to her as soon as possible, taking an hour-long cab ride. After six long hours she was let out, my mom and dad beside themselves with relief.

How does this relate to my mental health? First of all, it scared the crap out of me and made me ashamed that I had been the one who forgot to read the ingredients at the store. I was eleven at the time, but reading ingredients was a regular habit and rule for my family. Even when buying duplicates we'd read each label to ensure they weren't man-ufactured at different times or in a different facility with nuts. It got tedious. If this is something I did all the time, how could I have forgotten to read that one item? I could have killed my sister, and the guilt I felt was immense. Not that my family blamed me at all, they say my dad didn't read it either when he was with me as he was supposed to double-check, but I see no reason to fault him. It was me. In my head, everything was my fault.

The second way this affected me was that it made me hesitate to dial 911 a few times when I really should have called. If I didn't contact 911 for Lindsay, I wasn't going to call it for some petty reason like people breaking into my house to party. But I'll get to that later.

CHAPTER THREE

WHEN AUNT FLO BECOMES DEADLY

ENTERING HIGH SCHOOL was terrifying. I'm sure it is for everyone, but knowing that my grade school friends weren't in my classes and I'd be surrounded by strangers made my stomach drop. It certainly didn't help that I had severe acne with very oily skin, or a "pizza face" as I once heard in an acne commercial (thanks for the confidence boost!). I also had braces, glasses, frizzy dark blonde hair and a large nose that I hated. Does it get any better than that?

I had never had much self-confidence, but it definitely went downhill from my acne worsening with the advent of my period and nose growing with age. If I could barely look at myself, why would anyone else want to? I think this was the beginning of my self-hate. While I can't remember anyone ever making fun of me, I had enough emotional abuse from myself based on my looks and things I regretted doing earlier in life. Thankfully, I quickly made several friends, and felt completely comfortable being myself around them. Two of these new friends were Kayla and Vanessa, both incredibly sweet and always supportive. Most of us stayed great friends throughout high school, and some of us still got together in later years.

My period first came at the beginning of high school, causing my acne to explode from bothersome to uncontrollable. I went on a strong prescription pill for four months to help it, which it temporarily did, but it came back after a few months of being off the pill. I took it for two more rounds throughout high school with the same results each time—great skin, but only temporarily.

It was difficult to cope with the side effects. The first time I took this pill I had pain when walking and had much difficulty running. A lot of my hair fell out (not quite enough for others to notice) and I would have clumps of hair swirl down the drain when I showered. My oily skin became flaky and dry, and my acne diminished only a little.

I took monthly blood tests to ensure the drug wasn't destroying my liver, and I remember reading in the information I was given that it could possibly lead to depression. Who knows if it's true, or if that is what caused my constant depression later in life, but it's a possibility. The second and third times I was on the acne pill the symptoms were much milder, and I had clear skin going into university.

When I wasn't on this pill, my skin was very oily, like BP-oil-spill oily. Within fifteen minutes I'd have drops of oil all over my t-zone, especially on my nose, and within a half hour my whole face was an oil slick.

Before every class I would have to put a bunch of powder on my nose to try and control it and use tissues during class to "blow" my nose. This made me extremely self-conscious, always worried about the way I looked. Having oily skin accentuated my nose, at least to me, and there was no way of hiding it. Friends said that my nose suited me, but I didn't feel that it did in any way as I was a petite, shy girl, and my nose screamed "clown." In fact, one day we all got red clown noses to put on, and mine wouldn't even fit. Ugh, genetics.

—ee

I got lice in tenth grade thanks to Nicole, who unknowingly gave it to me. My family and I thought we were being so careful not to let her lice spread, but she couldn't help but do handstands and cartwheels around the house. Later that day, I was lying on a rug, crawling with her lice.

I discovered I had lice while sitting in front of my bedroom closet mirror, combing through my hair the morning of school picture day. I saw what I first thought was a small leaf in my comb. I scrunched my brows in confusion, then screamed in shock as I saw the leaf move. These bugs were all over my head. Crawling through my hair. I get shivers just thinking about it. And my head just got itchy writing about it. My parents came running into my room asking what the matter was. I began crying and trying to say that I had lice.

I spent the day off school so Mom could have time to go through my hair with a special lice comb, me lying cold and almost completely naked on a white sheet on my bedroom floor so as not to spread the lice. She carefully picked the large lice out first, then moved on to searching for eggs. It took at least an hour. This was our morning ritual for the next couple weeks. Our cold, naked ritual.

During that time I had thought of a natural alternative I could use that I read about online, which was using olive oil in my hair to smother the lice. Mom refused to let me do that, believing the oil would not come out of my hair. Little did we know that olive oil is great for hair. Instead, my mom gave me some chemical-laden shampoo that turned my hair into greasy straw. It felt and looked like straw but also appeared greasy, as if I hadn't been washing it.

Picture retake day arrived, and I had to get my photo taken. Crap, I thought. This is not going to go well. I did my best when applying my makeup, hoping it would take away from my hair, but that plan backfired.

The photo ended up being the worst looking photo I have ever had in school. Or anywhere. The slight blue eye-shadow I applied became vibrant from the camera, as did the berry lip gloss I had on. My skin was shiny from my oily skin, and my hair was shiny (not in a good way) and messy looking from the straw texture. All of this, coupled with acne and a large nose I didn't like, made me look like a clown. And there was no option for a retake, because that *was* the photo retake.

I had to go through a year of high school with that photo, looking at it with disgust, and seeing it on my student card. Every time I saw it I was reminded of how I did not like the way I looked. I was terrified of people having to see that picture of me in the school yearbook, and wondered if that's what I looked like every day. It was another hit to my self-esteem, which was already broken, and caused me to dislike myself even more.

Why am I so ugly? And not photogenic? I wish I didn't look the way I do. I know this is high school and it's normal for it to be an awkward stage of life, but come on. If I'm ever going to get any confidence it's not going to be with how I look. I am good at school…but does that really matter? I'm still stupid. I can't do anything right. God, I suck. Even worse, I hate that I get these negative thoughts when I should be happy with my life. I am happy, other than with myself, but not happy all the time. Not when my period comes.

—ꝯ⌒

One thing that brought out my negative thoughts was my period. It brought out violent thoughts, too. Not toward others, but toward myself. Always myself. No one or anything else was the problem, I was the problem. I just wanted to die. I would cry uncontrollably for hours most times, and others I would be numb. It would be so nice if I could just find the strength to kill myself, but I was weak. I wouldn't actually do it, I just wanted to. Badly.

I think it's important to note that I in no way associate strength or weakness with suicide, it was just the way my thoughts worked at this time.

I struggled with these emotions and thoughts of suicide for one to three days almost every month for years. This was normal to me. It was the only thing I had ever known, and I knew PMS caused women to become emotional. I even had it confirmed that it was normal when in the change room for a gym class:

"Oh, my god, I'm on my period, I just want to kill myself," said one girl.

"Me, too," others agreed.

I nodded my head along with the rest of the girls, agreeing that my period made me want to die and kill myself, not realizing it was an exaggeration on their part. They just meant that they hated the pain of menstrual cramps and their periods were bothersome, not that they wanted to literally kill themselves.

One night I couldn't take it anymore. Not to the point of killing myself—I still believed it was something I wouldn't do—but I could not stand feeling this way every fucking month. It was exhausting and something I'd continually dread. I didn't feel like me, as I became a shell of a person. I logged onto Yahoo Answers under a pseudonym, asking if it was normal to have suicidal thoughts during PMS. While writing this memoir, I was able to find what I wrote, from 2008, after a crap load of searching:

```
I doubt I'd actually hurt/kill
myself, but today, just like al-
most every other month (because
of pms), I had thoughts of sui-
cide. I was full of anger and
crying, tried my longest not to
eat, and just felt like everyone
including myself would be hap-
pier if I killed myself.

I'm feeling better now, just a
bit sad, but is this normal? I am
on birth control, so could that
have something to do with it? It
would be nice if there was a way
to stop it, because it scares me.

Thanks.
```

The eighteen answers I received were instantaneous, the majority of them telling me it was not normal and to seek help. Looking back at this submission, not thinking I would ever find what I wrote that day again, makes me feel empathy for that girl. Someone who is so scared that she wants to both die and keep going, conflicted about something that should be clear. I certainly wouldn't be happier if I killed myself, I'd just be gone. My family would be a wreck, friends would cry, and I wouldn't be able to have the impact on people I do today.

Receiving those responses immediately caused my eyes to water as they opened wider. I was shocked; the way I had been feeling for years wasn't normal. I didn't have to go through those wretched feelings every month. What those girls said in the change room didn't mean what I thought it did. Am I going to have to live the rest of my life like this? I used to think so, but now that I knew it shouldn't be this way I wanted to get rid of it. I didn't want to live this way anymore, it was painful. Emotionally and mentally. Even physically.

One of the answers to my question got me to look up a severe form of PMS called PMDD, or premenstrual dysphoric disorder. There were other women in various forums who had similar experiences and it felt nice to know I wasn't the only one. This is something I was never diagnosed with but I still believe it's what I have, though now kept in check thanks to the right birth control. What I do know for sure is that people just shouldn't feel the urge to kill themselves during PMS.

Some of what I read, though, was about women who experienced much anger and sadness for two weeks before their periods, which made me feel like my measly one to three days of depression and suicidal thoughts were trivial. Either way, I did not tell anyone about this, besides Melissa, until later in life.

Asking that online question was the first time I had told anyone about my bouts of period-related severe depression. It was something I had always kept to myself because I thought it was normal.

Until reading that post again, I'd forgotten about the anger I would hold inside. Anger at myself. Anger at a sister for doing something so minuscule, like not helping with the dishes, it should just warrant a bit of frustration. Anger at the world.

I also forgot that I would try to starve myself during these episodes, previously thinking I only did this during my full-on depression in the coming years. I wouldn't try to starve myself to die, but to punish myself for being who I was. When I don't eat I get an upset stomach and I have thrown up from this before. Throwing up with nothing in your stomach is awful, your lungs struggle for air as your stomach continually tries to heave up something that isn't there.

In addition to the upset stomach, as the hours go on, I get strong stomach pains that prevent me from standing straight, lightheadedness, pains through my whole upper body, and finally I become shaky and sweaty. If I wasn't going to kill myself, I reasoned, I needed some other way to punish myself, and starving myself seemed the easiest route.

This brings me to the birth control pill: something my body has never liked but needed. When I first got my period I had it for three months straight and went on birth control to stop it. I've had to stay on the pill ever since. I've also learned that I have quite high testosterone levels, which is one reason why my hormones are messed up. I tried a couple different types of birth control pills to stop spotting, but with each type I still had depressive episodes and suicidal thoughts.

One type left me numb, and scaring my family for two weeks until I went on a different pill. A gynecologist I saw said the birth control wasn't the cause of it, but I still think that's up for debate. When I was numb I remember sitting on a kitchen chair staring into space with watery eyes, my head void of anything. My dad wanted to bring me tobogganing with Nicole, but I didn't want to go because I'd rather just sit on the chair. After much persuasion I gave up and went with them, managing to elevate my mood a bit by going down the hills a couple times with a slight laugh or two.

Melissa called me one night in eleventh grade during my PMS and I burst out crying over the phone. I couldn't control my emotions and told her about what I was going through each month and how I didn't know for a long time it wasn't normal. I hid this from everyone else for a reason. I didn't want people to worry about me. I only felt like killing myself, I wasn't going to do it. What I didn't tell Melissa, or anyone for that matter, was how depressed I felt.

CHAPTER FOUR

WELCOME TO THE PIT OF HELL

I can't remember exactly how it happened. Did I become upset over time, depression sneaking up on me? Did it just never go away one month during PMS? Did it randomly hit me and just stay? Whatever the cause, I got depression at the beginning of my final year of high school. I thought I had experienced sadness before, but boy, was I ever wrong. Feeling like this felt like hell.

I spent those first few months of my final year in a deep depression. I hid it from everyone, including my family. I think they knew something was wrong, but they had no idea how bad it really was and frankly, I didn't want them to know. They couldn't find out I was hanging on by a thread.

There was a part of me that wondered if this was how I always was. Did I used to cry while spreading mustard on a sandwich? I couldn't remember. I have always been an emotional person, but maybe I was only more aware of it now. Now that the suicidal thoughts were there for more than a couple days of the month. Maybe this was how I was supposed to be feeling, a punishment for something. Why did I ever not want to kill myself? It became part of my normal thoughts and it seemed like a pretty good option. Sometimes like the only option.

Do it. You'll be miserable for the rest of your life if you don't. Fucking stupid, emotional fool.

For about five days a week I was seriously suicidal. The other couple days I would consider "happy" days, where I only sort of wanted to kill myself, and experienced some joy.

The sad days, they were sad. Really sad. Like, you think you've sunk to the bottom but there's farther to fall, kind of sad. It was as if there were a dark cloud over me. You've probably heard that before, but things were literally darker. My eyebrows would scrunch together and not be able to relax, and everything looked gloomy. If I was able to feel any joy, then things would become brighter and the muscles in my face would allow for everything to relax including the possibility of a smile.

With that darkness came negative thoughts. As I mentioned earlier, I did not have very good self-esteem and would frequently, if not always, talk negatively to and about myself. I began a new ritual every day of looking in the mirror and telling myself I was nothing. A blank-faced, depressed girl filled with inner turmoil stared back at me. "I am nothing," I would say and think. "I am disgusting," I would often add.

I became my own worst enemy, bullying myself into negative cycles of thinking. These became my core beliefs, beliefs so powerful that I thought it was impossible for anything else to be true.

With these negative thought patterns came suicidal thoughts, convincing me that I would be better off dead. That others would be better off without me, too. I would no longer be a burden and no one would care if I was gone. The only downfall I really saw was that I would have to go through physical pain in order to not be here anymore. There was also always a part of me that wondered if my family may miss me, and if so, could I do that to them?

Of course they won't miss you. For fuck's sake, stop being so selfish all the time. How can you seriously think that they would ever care about you? You feel like a burden for a reason: because you are one.

Being shy meant I had never liked going to school, but being depressed and going to school was even more difficult. As I slowly walked to the cafeteria to meet with my friends before classes started, I would sit down, stare at the ground and often not say anything. Any time they asked if I was alright, I just told them I was tired. This was true, but it was more than that. In addition to the exhaustion, in my head I was thinking about how desperately I wanted to die. Ways I could die. For the mental and emotional pain to end. To be rid of everything.

Then I would plaster a fake smile onto my face for my friends to see, as if everything were fine. I'd slowly walk up to my class on the third floor, feeling as if I were a ghost. I wasn't really there, was I? My mind was somewhere else completely, but my body went to school each day. During a spare, when I didn't have a class, I went to the library to study. But instead of getting anything done, I just started crying. Ugh, that was happening a lot. I would walk to the bathroom, pull myself together, and go on with the rest of my day.

Who knows how I did it, but I got great marks in twelfth grade just as I did every other year of school. This was with difficulty studying and eventually having to give it up. Studying worsened my suicidal thoughts, especially in math. I was already having difficulties concentrating, and doing calculus along with two other math courses gave me plenty of fuel to believe I wasn't good enough. Any problem I couldn't easily solve made me angry, upset, frustrated, and spiraled me out of control mentally. I just wanted to kill myself even more.

Way to go Michelle, you can't even do homework. You know that kids in kindergarten can do their homework, right? Why are you so pitiful? Don't even bother trying to do this anymore, you won't get any answers right. Your thinking is so screwed up lately and you have a shit memory, thanks to me; you're welcome. Good luck concentrating on anything. You're just going to be a high school dropout. Bye-bye to dreams of university. I doubt you'd even live that long, anyway. Just go to sleep, it's what you do best. I mean, really, all your attempts at homework are going down shit creek. Just sleep in that creek. Preferably face down.

I'd scribble over my mistakes until the pen went through the paper. I dropped my calculus course because I couldn't keep up with it without studying, but I forced myself to push through the others.

―ee―

While in twelfth grade I began driving lessons. They were not my cup of tea. I drove with an instructor most times, while others I'd drive with my dad. It was less scary with the instructor, knowing she had a brake pedal if it were ever needed. Driving made me the most anxious I had ever been. I could kill somebody with one wrong move. I didn't like the idea of people's lives being in my hands. I'd never forgive myself if I hurt someone.

My driving instructor taught me to be a cautious driver. I was already overly cautious. She made it known that I had to continually check my mirrors every few seconds, yet always keep my eyes on the road; be fully aware of every car and person around me; drive as if no one else knows how to drive, so prepare for anyone to make a wrong move at any second; check the speedometer often to make sure I was always near the speed limit but never over it. This put so much pressure on me that I became terrified of driving, and truthfully, I still hadn't learned some of the basics.

For example, no one had ever told me how to have your feet on the pedals. To keep your right foot straight over the brake and twist your foot to reach the gas. I always lifted my whole foot up, trying to guess where the heck it would go, wondering if at any second my foot would slip off because it wasn't fully on a pedal. I hated the feeling of worrying I may hit the wrong pedal, and once I did get the brake and gas mixed up, almost driving into a ditch with my dad and sister.

After that experience, the next time I got in the car my legs were shaking uncontrollably. I burst out crying, knowing I was a failure. I couldn't do anything right, not even drive a car. I had tried a couple other times to get in the car to drive but never left the driveway because who can drive with shaking legs and tear-filled eyes? My driving instructor had told me that she thought I was ready for the actual driving test, but I never booked it. If I couldn't trust myself driving, why should anyone else?

It's funny to me—in a not so funny way—that I was so terrified of hurting or killing someone that I couldn't drive, yet, I put no value on my own life. If I got hit by a car, fine, thank you and I'm gone. If I hit someone else, however, I'd never forgive myself for it. Likely kill myself as punishment for hurting or killing someone else. I can't stand knowing that other people can get hurt. No one deserves that—well, except for me.

—ℓℓ—

I went to a Catholic high school, which meant I occasionally needed to attend services. I'm not a religious person, let's get that out there, but I do have respect for religions and for those who are religious, as long as they show love and tolerance to everyone.

On one occasion in church, I was among seven other students who had to stand up at the pulpit to read a passage in front of everyone. We walked to the pulpit together in a row, me third from last, and began saying our passages one at a time. Let me add that we rehearsed beforehand, so we knew exactly where to stand and what to do after we spoke.

When it was my turn to read, I used a clear voice and didn't miss a beat. I turned around to walk to the back of the line…then kept on walking off the stage and back to my seat. For some reason I forgot I had to wait for the last two students to say their parts, and I noticed everyone staring at me. This had effectively interrupted the current speaker, and I felt horrible for messing up everything that we had practiced. It would have made things worse if I went back up onto the stage so I stayed seated, my body getting overly heated.

The heat kept increasing and my stomach felt like I was about to barf. Everything turned grey then black within several seconds, and my hearing was completely gone as well. Shit. I could feel the sweat dripping off of me, my heart rate increasing, and if I moved an inch I knew I'd puke all over the place. What am I supposed to do? I seriously feel like I'm going to faint. Oh, no, I already made a fool of myself, I don't need to do that all over again. I need to get to a bathroom or something, but how am I supposed to do that if I can't even see?

After a few minutes, my vision slowly returned and I could not only see a bit, I could also hear faint voices. I slowly turned my head to the boy beside me, who thankfully wanted to be a paramedic after high school, and told him I needed to go to the bathroom. He went with me, helping me stand up, my vision almost fully returned and my hearing nearly clear. He checked my eyes with a light and asked me various questions, ensuring that everything was getting back to normal. What on earth had just happened to me? I'd never experienced anything like that before and it was scary as hell.

I discovered a few days later at the doctor's office that I had experienced a panic attack. I was terrified of it happening again, not knowing when or where I could be set off. What if next time my hearing and/or eyesight didn't come back? Let's hope I never find out.

—ℓ—

I rarely, if ever, hung out with friends after school. It was something I didn't do very often anyway because of my social anxiety, but I became even less likely to do it because of my depression. I would come home after school and try to do homework, but it only intensified my suicidal thoughts so I'd give up pretty quickly.

After that, depending on my emotions, I would either lie on my bed and cry uncontrollably or sit on my desk chair and stare at the wall. Sometimes, if I was feeling a little better, I'd allow some light into my room and stare toward the window. Have you seen *New Moon*, the second movie in the *Twilight* series? In one scene the main character, Bella, sits on a chair and looks out the window with a dead gaze. That was me, and I lose it every time I watch that scene.

When I cried uncontrollably, it lasted for hours upon hours. It was as if I were drowning in my own tears, barely able to stay afloat. Trying to find my way out of the vast ocean that was my mind, but unable to see past the waves of despair. I desperately wanted to let go and get pulled into the darkness. I welcomed it.

I did my best to stay as quiet as possible, sometimes using a pillow to muffle the sobs. Perhaps my parents thought

I was doing homework for a long time, or was just being a typical teenager by staying in my room. I wouldn't dare let them find out how upset I was. They shouldn't have to deal with worrying about me.

My head hurt so much from all the sobbing, which exhausted me completely. When I wept (and sometimes to induce crying) I'd listen to depressing music. Linkin Park was my poison of choice, in addition to some songs from City and Colour. I listened to their songs on repeat, certain lines resonating with me and making me wish I could end it all. While the music made me cry more, it also allowed me some sort of release. As if someone else could understand what I was going through. Dark as it was, and though it sometimes made me want to hurt myself more, it also kept me here.

When depressed, my speech and comprehension were slower. I've always been slower at doing things than the average person, but this took it to another level. I remember one specific time when Dad asked me a question about the hockey game we were watching and it took me a few seconds to even understand what he was saying. I responded with a dead, sluggish voice. This was a common occurrence, unfortunately. I physically couldn't do anything quickly and I just wanted it all to end.

One way I could sort of end it all was by going to sleep. I'd go to bed as early as 8:00 p.m., both because I was almost always tired and because I didn't want to be awake. I would've gone to bed earlier but I didn't want to look too suspicious. Going to sleep each night I would hope and pray to a god I didn't believe in that I wouldn't wake up. To my disappointment, I woke up every morning. How is this even called living?

Every day I was exhausted. It was a struggle just to get out of bed. Showering was something I didn't want to have to do. Just walking left me fatigued. Standing was a struggle. Lying down was so much simpler, not requiring my energy and leaving me to feel helpless.

The stamina I did have went toward beating myself up mentally. I was helpless. I was also hopeless. I was worthless, pitiful, ugly, stupid, a complete waste of space and deserved to die. What else was I? Well, it would take forever for me to finish. That's why these negative thoughts never went away and were constantly spinning in my head. I believed them to my core, and no one would ever convince me otherwise.

I'm glad you're seeing things clearly. An idiot like you is worthless. Well, more than worthless. You know what you are: you're nothing. *If anyone tells you otherwise, they're lying.*

As I did during my extreme PMS, I would often stop eating. It never had to do with my weight, it had to do with how much I needed food to feel well. There were times that it went beyond mere self-punishment to trying to starve myself so I would die. I saw this as a big failure though, because I could never last even a whole day. The pain in my stomach would spread through my whole body, then came the other symptoms, the lightheadedness, shaking and sweating. I caved in every time by eating.

Sometimes I would try to hold my breath, hoping I could die that way. Again, I was a failure. I didn't even make it to the point of passing out (which I now know is what happens if you hold your breath—you can't die from it).

Another thing I would do was play a "game" with myself. If I left my room to walk down the hallway toward the bathroom and someone was there, then I would kill myself. If no one was around, then I'd go to the bathroom and wait another time. There were some days when someone would be walking in the hallway, and then the game would change: If it happened again that day I would do it. It never happened.

Leaving my room at all was difficult, and one time I seriously considered either peeing in my bed or in my garbage can. That was how badly I didn't want to leave my room. But then, if I played my game, maybe I'd be lucky enough to die.

I also did things to put my life at risk: I stopped looking both ways when I crossed the street, when walking with someone I'd walk on the side where the cars were, and if I took the subway (in Toronto) I walked the yellow line of the platform; all hoping that something would happen to me and bring me the death I so wished for.

There were several other things I did to put myself in danger but honestly, I'm testing my memory by writing this. So much of my life in those years are cloudy, but I'm doing my best to push through that fog for this memoir.

I'd always think about how much easier things would be if I had access to a gun. It would be instant, just one click. But also permanent. Is that what I wanted? I had frequent fantasies of ending my life by shooting or hanging. This is what I'd daydream about: not my future, or a cute guy, but death.

Trust me, it's what you want.

At about 2:00 a.m. one night in my bedroom during this depression, I decided I had to end it all. It was too much. Too much guilt, too much sadness, too much anger, pain, hopelessness, defeat and just everything. I hated myself. I hated myself to the point that I wanted to leave this world. Needed to. Walking to my computer, I logged onto Facebook. With heavy hands, I began typing my goodbye in a private message to Lindsay. I needed to say bye to someone. But I couldn't hit send. What if she saw it and I changed my mind? I didn't want anyone to know what I was going through and make people worry about me.

Instead I went to the bathroom, crying my heart out, trying to be quiet enough so no one could hear. The weeping was so strong that my shaking legs gave out and I fell onto the cold tile. Lying there, thoughts of suicide and self-hate racing in my head, I felt I had reached rock bottom. I had given up.

Ten long minutes I spent on that floor, desperately wailing, curled into a ball, sure that this was the end. But then…I didn't have a plan! How would I go through with this? Shit, why didn't I think of this earlier? Was I really ready for this if I hadn't even thought things through that far? I needed a way out but decided to wait until the morning. Then I would decide what to do.

You'd better do this tomorrow, though. Don't you dare chicken out. I'll let you wait that short while, but then it's time to end things. Who knows, maybe your shit self will get lucky and not wake up. Don't get your hopes up, though. You haven't done anything worthwhile to deserve that kind of good fortune. All you do is feel sorry for yourself while there are people starving around the world. And you're here trying to starve yourself. What a waste of time and space. Seriously, you are a waste of space. Remember that. I know your memory has been a piece of shit lately, but keep that tidbit in mind. Waste. Of. Space.

I knew the voice in my head was right. Using the counter, I slowly lifted myself back onto my feet, doing my best to stay quiet as I opened the bathroom door to the hallway. I couldn't let anyone know what I was thinking about doing tomorrow. They'd probably try to stop me.

I went to bed that night thinking it was over, but the next morning I felt a little better. Not enough that I didn't want to end my life, but enough that I felt I wasn't ready. I deleted the Facebook message I was going to send to my sister. Maybe another time. That voice in my head had settled down, leaving some rational thoughts in its place.

That was how it usually worked with me. I woke up disappointed I was still here, but with a semblance of hope, but throughout the day, every day, my thoughts got to me and I spiraled down to the point where I needed to sleep because being awake was misery. Part of me wanted to continue to feel depressed because it was what I deserved.

I encircled myself with guilt. Guilt for being depressed when other people had real problems. Guilt for doing something wrong, even if that wasn't the case. I'd go over every conversation I had with others, finding mistakes I made. I was also blameworthy for other times when I didn't talk to people because of my shyness. Everything was wrong.

—ee—

I can't remember what brought it on, but I sat down with my parents one day and they asked me how bad I was feeling. If I was having suicidal thoughts. I carefully nodded my head yes. Tears ran down my face as we hugged, my parents telling me that we'd work through it. This is when my mom revealed to me that she had experienced depression and anxiety. We immediately made an appointment with my doctor, Dr. Rodney, to see what could be done.

In his office, I was asked to fill out a depression checklist of my symptoms and rate them from not happening at all to occurring frequently. When I wrote my answers,

I was thinking that since I had a couple days out of the week during which I felt "normal," that the frequently section didn't apply to me. I didn't desperately want to kill myself all the time, so I answered "every once in a while."

When I handed it in I was diagnosed with mild depression. Not even Dr. Rodney knew how bad I really was. He suggested I start with healthy eating, exercise, and cognitive behavioural therapy (CBT). I'm glad he went to these options first from what he could tell about my symptoms. In hindsight, it would have been better to go on medication right away, in addition to these natural methods, because my life was at risk.

I tried eating healthier, I was able to manage a small amount of exercise, and I purchased a CBT book, reading a fair bit of it. I couldn't bring myself to do any of the CBT exercises, though, because they made me feel stupid. Like writing in a journal, which for some reason always made me feel silly. Why am I writing to myself? I already have thoughts in my head, I don't need to write them down. I once tried writing in a journal while depressed, and all I got out was a large "fuck you" with violent scribbles going through the page.

I went back to Dr. Rodney a few weeks later to let him know there was no improvement and he put me on an antidepressant. Knowing I was on medication for depression caused mixed emotions. Part of me was thinking, this means I'm officially so low I need the help of meds. Was I going to have to be on it for rest of my life? What about the side effects? I didn't want to experience increased sui-

cidal thoughts, which was a possibility, but without medication I would be gone for sure from hurting myself. But
another side of me was glad I was taking something that
could help my moods.

The side effects were not the greatest, but they also
weren't the worst. What I remember most was feeling rest-
less, like I was crawling out of my skin. I dug my feet into
the couch, Lindsay telling me to stop because it was an-
noying. But I didn't know how to stop, I felt so weird. I
also had a headache and felt a bit dizzy, but again, not so
bad. Future medication would be a doozy, though.

After just a couple of weeks I noticed a bit of a difference. Truthfully, it was my family that noticed first, but
when they brought it to my attention I could see it as
well. I was smiling more, talking more, staying up later,
and having milder suicidal thoughts. Soon those thoughts
were gone, and things were going well. But I fell back into
a depression after about a month. I had my medication
increased and I also began seeing a psychotherapist.

At the beginning of my first appointment, she asked
me what my biggest fear was. I told her there were two:
people and spiders. I felt so weird telling her this, thinking it's ridiculous that someone could be afraid of people.
Mind you, at this time I still didn't know that social anxiety existed. As for the spiders, they've always been creepy
to me. It's those legs that give me shivers.

I had a fair number of appointments with her, learning
about my fight or flight response and more. Then within
the next few months I had another relapse into depres-

sion. An antidepressant was added to the one I was on and again, it helped a bit.

This became a pattern and I had trouble going back to Dr. Rodney for an increase or change in medicine each time. I would think I was doing well when I really wasn't. I would cancel appointments because of a happy day, but then the next day I'd be depressed again.

My family was so supportive and I'm forever grateful to have them in my life. They stuck with me through the blank, empty stares, and through the tears. When walking down the hallway crying one day, I started falling because my emotions were too intense. My dad caught me and told me we'd get through this. My parents' love for me is unconditional, as is my love for them. They would try to engage me in conversation, invite me to spend time with them, and always let me know they were there. I know it scared them to see me the way I was, but they are some of the toughest people I know.

Depression distorts your thoughts so much. I could see no value in my life, but my sister Nicole did. When she was depressed, she saw no value in hers, but I saw a remarkable girl who had a whole life ahead of her. She recovered much faster than I did, making me proud of her, yet also jealous. Why couldn't I get through it, too?

By the time graduation and prom rolled around, I was feeling happy again thanks to another medication change. I managed to be on the honour roll for all four years of high school, which meant I had over an eighty percent average each year. Even my depressed year.

I hosted an after-prom party in my backyard, a group of about fifteen of us laughing around the fire pit, and listening to one of them play the guitar. My medication was effective and though I was excited for what the future would hold, I was also fearful my depression might return.

That summer I worked longer hours on a job where I had previously only worked four hours a week during the school year. Though I was always nervous at work and fearful I may get fired, I still enjoyed working there. Things were going well and I was ready to head to Brock University in the fall for a Bachelor of Business Administration degree.

CHAPTER FIVE

THE BEGINNING OR THE END?

MOVING TO UNIVERSITY was far scarier than going to high school. There were only a couple people I knew going to Brock University, none of whom were in my program or residence. I had a single room with a bathroom attached to another single room, and meeting my bathroom-mate, Hannah, relieved some of my fears. She was super kind and easy going, making me feel as comfortable as I could in that situation. After everything was put in my room and my parents had left, it was time to mingle with all the other students in the common room.

All of us introduced ourselves by going around in a circle and I tried to find people who seemed like we may click. I didn't find anyone right away, and it was time to head outside for a barbecue. On a bench together was a group of girls that I recognized from my floor—Erin, Julia, Heather, Melanie, and Hannah—that I sat with and we all instantly bonded. I had found "my people."

Going back to our rooms, I visited Hannah to let her know that I was on depression medication in case she ever saw the pills or noticed that I seemed sad. That was part of the truth. What part I never told her was that I also didn't know if I would become severely depressed again or if she might find my body dead on the floor. I didn't want her to freak out. So although I felt happy, there was still a very real part of me that believed I was capable of killing myself if I became depressed again. Quite a large part of me.

Still in our first week of university, my group of friends and I decided to join some of the orientation week activities. One of these was a Condom Poker event, for which we paid a few bucks for a bag of condoms instead of the typical chips. None of us played poker, but there was a plethora of other casino games that we got into.

We were so caught up in the fun and loading up on condoms that we stayed until staff began shutting it down. With all the condoms left behind the tables, staff members began giving us large handfuls of condoms rather than throwing them out.

Our bags were stuffed to the max and we walked over to a prize table to trade in our loot for something we could really use. Only one of us had a boyfriend and I wouldn't trust a no-name condom brand that had been shuffled around all night, anyway. We had enough condoms for all of us to get free shirts and other Brock swag, while still each having a bag of leftover ones.

We swiftly made it over to the bingo area where they were getting rid of extra pens they had, and those lasted me for a couple years. Finally, with little time to spare, we collected the helium balloons—that we later inhaled— and took a picture to commemorate the night. I had no idea university would be so amazing so soon.

—ℓ

Then about a week later my depression came back and hit hard. The girl who was sincerely laughing and having a blast several days ago disappeared. There was no reason for it. No reason to be depressed when I wasn't even feel- ing homesick. No reason to feel blue when I had made genuine friends so quickly. I was suicidal. I would have daydreams about jumping out my fourth-floor window. As if that were a good thing.

I had told a couple friends about my suicidal thoughts returning, including Vanessa from high school, who made me promise to contact her if these thoughts escalated. I agreed to do so, even though I wasn't positive if it was a promise I could keep.

I attended my lectures and even made friends in some of them, but I wasn't happy anymore. I did virtually no homework, only working on necessary assignments. I knew my suicidal thoughts would get worse if I did schoolwork. It was common for me to be frustrated and have difficulty concentrating on assignments, but one night I couldn't handle it and threw my textbook at the wall across the room. I had enough. In other words, I cried and went to bed in hopes of disappearing.

You can disappear and you will. I know what's best for you. You can stop wasting the oxygen that other people need. You just have to get the guts to do it.

My marks weren't what they used to be. Instead of being in the eighties and nineties, I was most often in the sixties. That shouldn't have come as a surprise though, considering I could barely do homework and had difficulties concentrating on assignments. Thankfully, Hannah was a genius when it came to math and she was able to help me when I was struggling with statistics and calculus.

Because I was socially anxious, I never ate in the cafeteria if none of my close friends were there. This meant that sometimes for dinner, if our times didn't mesh, I ended up just eating snacks in my room. For lunch I was usually alone, so I always bought something I could carry and eat upstairs in my room. There was no way I was going to be seen sitting alone in a cafeteria, just as I could never do that in high school. It would bring me too much negative attention.

—ะ๛

There were times I would think I should see Dr. Rodney and I would make an appointment, but then, just as in high school, I would feel better for two or three days and cancel it. There was no point in seeing the doctor if I was having happy days, right? I didn't want to waste his time. Other people were more important than me. I was just a depressed girl with no real problems. Maybe these couple happy days meant there were more to come.

Things didn't get better though, they got worse. I couldn't handle it anymore. I couldn't be here anymore. It was all too much. I felt even more depressed than the last time I had thought like this. I just don't get how I got here. Nothing in my life was bad. I had a great life, a great family, and great friends. All fucking great. I'm the fuck up. There's no other explanation. I am a waste of space. I haven't forgotten. I know this is true.

How much more pathetic can you get? Perfect Michelle has money to go to university and get what she wants. Pa-the-tic. Seriously, how can you live with yourself? That's right, you don't. You just wallow in your sadness. Boo-fuckin'-hoo. Toughen up, sunshine, and do something about it.

"I'm too afraid, it's going to hurt," my mind mocks me. *You know who thinks that? Weak people. Like you. Just think about it. Is there any purpose to your life? Would anyone miss you? Do you even care a bit about yourself? The answer is no. No matter how many times you think this through, you're go-*

ing to come to the same conclusion. That this is it. It won't get better. This is your life. Pitiful as it is. Just kill yourself. Things will be easier that way, trust me.

This was my end. I deserved it, though. I was a fucking failure, I was a bad person for things I had done in my past, everything I did was *wrong. All fucking wrong.* There was nothing right with me, I was disgusting and nothing and stupid and full of shit the way I acted around people, pretending to be fine when all I wanted was to kill myself. I was selfish for wanting to do this, but at the same time, what gave me the right to think that anyone would miss me?

How fucking selfish of you to think that anyone would miss you. You are a worthless piece of shit. You are pathetic. Everything you are is nothing. You are nothing. *Why can't you get that through your fucking skull?! I know you're better off dead. Everyone would be happier if you were dead. Stop being a burden and fucking do something. You've failed before, don't do it again. Finally do something right. Kill yourself. Do you hear me, you fucking idiot?!*

Kill yourself.
Now.
Fucking do it.

I opened Google and searched all the possible ways I could kill myself, preferably with the least pain because

I was weak, and it needed to be something that would for sure finish me off and not leave me as a vegetable. If I failed my attempt and didn't have the ability to do it again, that would be the worst-case scenario.

What are my options...Jump out of the window? Sounds like a good idea, but I worry that it's not high enough and I don't want students to be scarred from seeing my broken, bloody body on the ground outside.

Hanging? I don't know where I'd get a rope or belt or even where I would hang it from.

Overdose on pills? I have loads of my prescription medication and a bunch of Advil, Tylenol, and other pills...this is definitely an option. The only downfall is I may throw them up or pass out and not die, but that gives me a second chance to get it done, no vegetable.

Drink bathroom cleaner? No, that would erode my esophagus.

Carbon monoxide? Now this sounds ideal but how would I do it...The best option is to run a car in a garage with all the doors closed. Damn. I could certainly get the keys to the car even though I was too fucking scared to drive and get a license, and all I had to do was turn it on and make sure there were no cracks in the garage door not only for me, but mostly so it wouldn't get into the rest of the house. I couldn't allow anyone else to get hurt, only me. Though this all sounded so perfect, I would have to wait until the next time I got home and that would take way too long. I need to go now. Not home to the garage, but I need to get off this earth.

My second-best option is the pills. Pills it is. I closed my computer and wiped away my tears.

Oh, my god. I'm going to do this. I'm actually going to do this. Oh, shit. What if it's the wrong decision? I can't go back on it, but it's something I know I need to do. Fuck, I want this so badly but I'm worried that my family might care about me. Could they? Is it possible that they may miss me or would they just feel sorry for me? Oh, god, I don't know if I can do that to them. But they don't. They don't care. They will be happier without me here. This will be helping them.

I want this so badly. *So* badly. I want this more than I've wanted anything in my life. If I can't have happiness, can I not just have this? The tears I wiped away returned. Returned with a vengeance. I fall down on my bed bawling my eyes out, hands behind my back, shaking and hyperventilating from the force of my crying. Knees bent in the air with my feet pounding and digging into the bed. Biting my lip, trying but failing to be quiet. I wanted to reach for those pills in my drawer. I *needed* to reach for those pills, I thought, as my eyes fixated on them through the drawer and through my tears.

Fuck. Do you see how stupid you are, all you do is lie here and cry, hiding your hands as if that's going to do anything. Take the fucking pills! What the hell is wrong with you? Nobody gives a shit about you and it's about time you understand that.

As I get up to move toward the pills, a thought crosses my mind. Is there a chance my family might care? No, there's no way they could care about me, I'm *me*. That says everything. I want them to be happy, and I know they'll be happier with me gone.

Oh, shit. I promised Vanessa, a friend from high school, a couple months earlier that if I ever decided to kill myself I had to talk to her first. Fuck, I can't break that promise. Oh, god, this is it. At least I get to say goodbye to someone. She was a great friend. I can't believe this is the end, but it's better this way. I fulfill the promise and I kill myself. Done deal.

As I begin to dial her number, something comes over me. A feeling I've never felt before. I begin crying more than I ever had in the past, if that's even possible, pushing all the life out of me in a different way. Fuck, she cares. What if my family cares? Vanessa wants me to call because she's concerned. Or because she feels bad for me. What if this is the wrong decision? I can't do this right now if I'm not totally sure. I can't risk my family getting hurt from my decisions. I know the odds of them caring are minuscule, but there's still a chance.

I hung up the phone and sent Vanessa a text. I told her that I almost killed myself but felt some relief as soon as I began typing her number. I thanked her. I need to thank her again. I haven't talked to her in years, but I want her to know that she helped save my life. That the only rational thought left in my head, no matter how small, and the promise I made to Vanessa, were enough to keep me alive. I cannot hurt my family. And this would hurt them. Though I'd be happier gone, I can't let them be sad so I'll stay. For now, I'll stay.

The rest of that day was spent crying until I fell asleep. Though many of my nights were like this, this one was different. I had almost taken my own life. The next morning came and I was glad I made the decision I did. I was still depressed, that was no question, but I no longer felt that I needed to kill myself. It was just a want. A big want, but not a need. I mean, I figured I'd probably end up dying by suicide, but not then. Not yet.

Now that there are more rational thoughts in my head, I have to tell my parents that I need to see Dr. Rodney again. No more cancelling if I have a happy day, because if there's one more day like yesterday I will be gone. There's only so long I can hold on. It's exhausting being depressed. Every day it feels like you've run a marathon, but all I ever did was lie in bed and cry or stare into space. Life like that is just existing, not living.

I didn't tell any of my friends about what happened. I kept going as if everything were the same, but I did tell my parents I came close to hurting myself and made an appointment with my doctor. I got a medication change and it was able to keep me going through university. Not enough to keep away the depression, but enough to keep away the hindering suicidal thoughts.

I decided to take up running to aid my mental health. It wasn't your typical running though, it was the socially anxious version. I'd lock my dorm room and bathroom doors to ensure no one could enter, put in my earphones, and begin running on the spot. I'd run for about twenty minutes every night, rarely missing a day and always breaking a sweat. This way I could exercise with no one seeing me and head straight to the shower afterward to clean off.

—ᴇᴇ—

One night while hanging out with my close friends in Erin's room down the hall, I told them that I had depression. It took a while to get the words out, but the moment I did I felt relief. It hurt to hide this from them for so long, and telling them made me feel lighter. In turn, I found out that a few of them had experienced anxiety and/or depression. Though I knew mental illness was fairly common, it was surprising to find out that people I thought I knew so well had these illnesses. They probably thought the same thing about me.

Since we all got along so well, we decided to find a house to live in together. We went as a group to visit different houses, which made me feel more comfortable than if we had gone individually.

The first house we visited was a pig sty. It smelled of must, dirty dishes, and stale air. When we walked in we were asked to leave our shoes on. As if we were even thinking of taking them off. There was a rotting chicken carcass thick with flies on the microwave in the kitchen, dishes everywhere, and a half-eaten package of hotdogs lying open on a tenant's dresser, with a joint lying around. We thanked the landlord for the tour, leaving as soon as we could. This wasn't a good sign for future houses.

The following house we saw had bedrooms in the basement with no windows and there was mold inching across the basement ceiling. The next had mouse poop, mouse traps, and Cheetos crumbs all over the floors. Almost ready to give up our search, we finally found a great basement apartment that was spacious and clean with six bedrooms. And we were asked to take our shoes *off.* I was really looking forward to living there with my best friends.

I made it through the rest of first year and even got a job for the summer in Toronto at a call centre giving directions to customers. This was going to be a summer where I would really have to push myself. You see, I'm afraid of talking on the phone. I stare at it while it rings and try to force myself to pick it up. I also try to avoid making calls. In addition to this, I've always been bad with directions. If you bring me to my hometown of sixteen years and get me to take you around, I'll barely know where to go. Yet here I was, at a job requiring me to do all these things.

Despite these minor issues, I wanted to prove to myself that I could practice hard enough on both the phone calls and directions, and hopefully be comfortable with both by the end of the summer.

Most days while working I was happy, but there were some that I was depressed. This was especially difficult being in a customer service position, having to fake a smile and make my voice sound happy. A couple days I even had to call in sick to work, unable to stop crying.

Though I was happy most days, I was also often afraid of being fired. It lingered in the back of my mind. I was always worried about doing something wrong, saying something wrong, working too slowly, messing up directions, and more. I had this same fear at my previous job. I just wasn't confident enough in myself. That voice in my head was telling me that I wasn't good enough and I often listened to it.

Early that summer my supervisor called me over to let me know the company received a letter from a customer who had been given the wrong directions and missed a job interview. I told my supervisor I didn't think it was me, but she confirmed she had listened to a recording of the phone call. What happened was that I read the schedule backwards. I was devastated. I felt horrible for that woman, awful that I had marred the company's reputation, and embarrassed that I could've made such a stupid mistake.

I turned around with glassy eyes to go back to my seat, the other supervisor gazing at me with empathy. The rest of the day I spent doing all I could to hold back my tears. Thinking of jokes, thinking of funny experiences, anything. At least this taught me a good lesson, to always double check information with a customer.

By the end of the summer I was told that I had greatly improved over the months, which helped me feel better about my time spent there. I had become more comfortable talking on the phone. It still made me a bit nervous, but not nearly as anxious as it used to. I also greatly improved my knowledge of directions, at least with what I was taught for the job. Otherwise, my sense of direction still sucks.

During this time I spent about half the summer living with Lindsay in her condo. One morning I heard an alarm going off, but it wasn't the fire alarm (I knew this from experience—it's not fun running down dozens of flights of stairs). This got me wondering what the sound could mean, and I was disoriented because it had just woke me up.

No one else was home and I didn't know what to do. I was paranoid. What if someone had got into the building and security was trying to warn people? Oh, god, someone's going to try and break in. What else could this alarm be for? What can I do? Hide? No, they'd find me. Ok, what can I do…grab my phone. Yes, keep my phone on me. What else…there are knives in the kitchen, that would surely scare them off and protect me if I absolutely had to use one. I heard the sound of the elevator and looked through the peep hole. Oh, god, who is it?

Lindsay's face appeared on the other end and I sighed in relief. Everything was fine. Crap, I had put the dead bolt on in my haste and she won't be able to get in with just her key. I unlocked both locks and opened the door.

My sister stared at me in fear and started yelling at me. Oh, god, I'm still holding a knife in one hand and a phone in the other. Shit. Shit, shit, shit.

She ordered me to put the knife away, which I would have done anyway, and kept yelling, asking what the hell I was thinking and going to do with it. I told her what I thought, and she immediately called my dad who was in the same city. I swore to Lindsay I would never, ever hurt her or anyone else. She had trouble believing me from all the shock, and my dad arrived soon after.

We came to an understanding that I had let my mind run off in paranoia, envisioning the worst possible scenario. I still don't know what caused that alarm, but it was likely someone testing their alarm system. Continuously.

The guilt I felt after that incident was so strong, and lasted for years. How could I ever come back from this and have a good relationship with my sister again? Will she even let me back in her condo?

She did let me stay at her place whenever I wanted to for the rest of the summer, but I had trouble pretending that nothing had happened. It was something I desperately wanted to take back or at least forget about, but it wouldn't leave me. I was fearful of using knives around her for years afterward and I still think about it every time I take knives out of the dishwasher, walking past people with the knives covered by my hand.

The way my mind worked that morning actually wasn't how it normally does. I do tend to either overreact or under-react, but most often it's an under-reaction. Heck, while working that summer it was the G20 Toronto summit in which the only people I saw on my way to work were cops on each street corner. Not even any cars. It was complete silence other than the wind. Once in my building, I had to pass the security clearance and head straight to the elevators.

In the middle of the day, we were told the building was on lockdown because of the nearby riots. People were out of control, smashing building windows and setting police cars on fire. I sat in the break room eating a bagel and someone came in to repeat the news. They wondered why I was so calm. My response was, what can I do? I trust the security, I'm just going to enjoy this bagel, it was free. The next day we had to move to a building farther away for our safety and still, I was chill as can be.

CHAPTER SIX

HOW DOES ONE HANDLE THEIR FEARS?

SOON AFTER GOING back to university for my second year, I began thinking about switching programs. Not the best thoughts to have, but they sure as hell are better than suicidal thoughts. Thumbs up for me.

Unfortunately, I no longer had the passion for business that I previously did. Before, I would enjoy thinking about ways people could be persuaded or manipulated through advertising and marketing, but now I wanted to reveal the truths of these companies. I wanted to learn about social problems and how they could be fixed, I wanted to learn about oppression, I wanted to make a positive difference in the world. I was too afraid of making the switch though, because it meant I would fall behind and not graduate with my friends. I let this idea simmer for a couple months.

One change I did make right away, was a switch to vegetarianism. This decision had been percolating slowly throughout the years, but my meat eating finally came to a halt when I was eating a frozen dinner with chicken. My chewing slowed down and my face scrunched up, disgusted at what I was eating. I spit out my food and threw the rest out, knowing it was something I could no longer eat.

The next week I ate chicken noodle soup, taking out the chicken, ignorant of the fact that it's made with chicken broth. After a couple weeks I got the hang of things. I still enjoyed the smell of meat so it didn't bother me when housemates were cooking, but it did get a bit tedious answering questions like, "But what about the plants?"

Being vegetarian is something that makes me slightly uncomfortable in social situations, when I have to decline certain foods or double check to make sure there is no meat in a dish. I know it's not the same as an allergy, especially since I have a sister with one, but perhaps you can think of it as the possibility of bugs in your food. Wouldn't you want to double check that a bunch of cockroaches hadn't been cooked into your meal? To me, though, it's closer to finding bits of human in your food. No need to agree with me, I just feel that we're closer to animals than we allow ourselves to think.

In addition to the vegetarianism, I chose to eat healthier in general. I knew it would be good for my mental health so now was the perfect time to start.

I didn't allow myself to buy any unhealthy food. Most items were perishable, and I seldom ate prepackaged or processed foods. I stuck to mostly whole wheat pasta, fruit and vegetables. My housemates once saw me eating a sugary cereal and were all shocked, never having seen me eat that way before. That's how healthy I ate while living with them.

I would still get cravings for unhealthy foods at times, but I made sure never to get anything bad for me during my grocery runs. That way during cravings I'd be too lazy to go out just to grab a pizza or ice cream, so I'd snack on an apple instead.

In addition to laziness, I also had a fear of going grocery shopping. Walking into the store is fine, but my eyes go directly to the shopping carts. I hated how they made me feel as if I couldn't blend in, even though most people use carts while shopping. They get heavy, harder to turn and control, and my temperature slowly rises. I once ran over a woman's foot during a busy night and apologized to her profusely. That just added to my nerves in the future.

When I wait in line for groceries, even if it's the self-checkout lane (which I usually choose), my body heats up immensely, just as it does in any other store. But for groceries, I'm buying a lot more than I would anywhere else, meaning I have to stay there longer. By the time all my food is packed into bags I am dripping sweat down my face, trying unsuccessfully to hide it from everyone. Although no one has ever said anything to me about it, I know it's obvious.

Then I do my best to haul the bulging, heavy bags on my shoulders, elbows, and hands to make it onto the bus, and this does not bode well for my body heat. What gets me through it all is knowing food is a necessity and that once I make it home I can cool down and not have to worry about it for at least a week or two.

—ꝰ—

After a few weeks of classes, one of them finance, I was trying my best to do homework but was experiencing difficulty again. The fear in me of becoming suicidal once more was so great that homework felt like a death sentence, but I did my best to push through a bit. Oh, god, please don't get depressed. I don't know if I can handle it. If I get too upset and frustrated I know where that could lead me. I'd be gone.

While in a finance lecture, trying to keep up after not having done much of the homework, I had my legs crossed and one leg and foot fell asleep. A break was announced and as I got up I stumbled and grabbed onto the table. My leg and foot were in full-on sleep mode.

I didn't want to look weird just standing there so I took a step, and my leg acted as if there was no foot at the bottom of it. My foot twisted to the side, almost completely sideways, and I heard a series of cracks. I couldn't feel any pain, though, because my foot was asleep. I stood on the other leg, waiting for my sleeping foot to regain feeling, and then the pain was immense.

I hobbled over to a seat in the hallway outside the classroom and got out a granola bar to look normal, not like I was just sitting there in agony. As my anxiety increased, the more things began to happen. I was burning hot, stomach ready to vomit, my hearing disappeared, and so did my eyesight. I felt extremely faint, but did all I could to hold on to where I was. I remembered I was holding a granola bar, so to appear normal I decided to eat it. I couldn't find my mouth. I felt the granola bar hit my chest, chin, and cheek before I gave up.

After a couple minutes my hearing began to return but it was as if I were underwater, and my vision was slowly coming back as well. My stomach was less upset, and I was covered in sweat. Whoa, I think I just had a panic attack like I did once back in high school. I slowly got up and walked to the bathroom in pain from my foot, rinsed off my face, and made my way home, limping. No way could I go back to class after that.

By the time I got home I could no longer put any weight on my foot, I had to hop. I called a cab and went to the hospital, hopping through the emergency room. The x-rays showed I had broken my foot and I was put in a giant cast and given crutches. I call them death traps. For someone who's already clumsy, crutches aren't the best help. They got me where I needed to go, but a hundred times slower.

I contacted my family, letting them know what had happened. Lindsay believed for the longest time that I was lying and it was a drunken accident. Nope. It was a sitting-in-class accident.

The next day I tried walking to the bus stop on my crutches, but instead of taking a maximum of three minutes it took me over fifteen. I could barely even make it onto the bus. This wasn't going to work. To get to my classes I ended up using a cab to and from school, missing a few classes to save money.

Being at school on crutches was extremely embarrassing, not only because it brought more attention to me but also because I felt like I looked stupid while walking with them. I could barely put one crutch in front of the other. Or, should I say, two crutches in front of my foot. They left me with bruised armpits, and at home I resorted to crawling and hopping, getting bruises on my knees but one leg of steel.

I was so relieved when I finally went to a doctor to get my cast taken off. I could walk again. Unfortunately for me, I forgot to bring a shoe for my healed foot. All I had on now was a tensor bandage. And it was raining. I really didn't want to have to use crutches any longer than necessary, but I had a class I needed to get to. I used the crutches to the cab, got a ride to school, and once inside the building I walked on my shoeless foot.

Making it to the campus store before class, I bought something small and used the bag they gave me to tie my foot in it. I walked around the school in my little bag bootie and even wore it walking home in the rain. Yes, it was embarrassing, but I felt that it brought less attention to me than crutches. Taking that bag bootie off felt like I was finally free. I could look normal once more and walk properly. Within a week, I got hit by a car.

—ℓ—

I was on my way to the bus stop for my night class. It was dark and I was walking through a rainstorm. I purposefully wore a vibrant white and pink polka dot bag so I'd be visible to cars. Good help that was.

I walked across the street at the green light, noticing that a car ahead of me to the right didn't look like it was going to stop. I was halfway through the road already. If I went backward a car turning left may not see me. If I moved forward, there was no way the driver ahead could miss me. I walked forward, the car not stopping. I froze in fear, peering through the windshield but unable to see through to the driver, and the car knocked me over and I landed on my side. Oh, shit. As I lay there on the wet, dirty asphalt, I thought, *this is it*. I'm about to feel the tires and die. I squeezed my eyes shut but didn't feel anything other than the pain of the fall.

I got up, now able to see the driver staring back at me in shock through the windshield. I can only assume she was texting when she hit me. How else could you explain what happened? Her eyes must have been on her fucking phone. I was so angry, looked at her in disgust, and continued walking, well, now hobbling, to the bus stop with tears in my eyes and an aching leg.

She rounded the corner of the street and put a window down, asking me to come to her car. Yes, make the injured girl walk toward you so your hair doesn't get wet. I walked up to the car and she apologized, saying she could drive me to school. I wasn't getting in a car with her. I said no, it's fine, but I was obviously angry and beginning to cry.

I never thought to get her license plate, car make, or anything. I was busy wondering how many people had seen that happen and what they were thinking. She drove away, and I never saw her again.

No longer able to control my crying, I changed directions and walked home. With difficulty. When I got in the door I burst into tears, my housemates stopping their cooking and asking what was wrong.

"I got hit by a car," I bawled as my rain-covered glasses fogged up, telling my friends the whole story.

Within a half hour I could no longer put any pressure on my leg, the pain in my knee unbearable. Off to the hospital again. This time a couple of my housemates went with me, waiting hours in the emergency room. While taking x-rays of my knee I could barely sit on the hard metal table, realizing there was tenderness in my hip. No break this time though, just a sprained knee. I had to use my crutches again since I couldn't walk on my own. The next day I woke up feeling like I was hit by a truck. Or a car. You couldn't see any bruising, but half my body felt completely bruised and beaten up. I could barely move.

That's when I remembered I hadn't told my parents about what happened. It wasn't that big of a deal though, so I just sent them an email saying I "sort of" got hit by a car. That didn't go over too well. They called immediately, asking if I was okay, and I let them know I was doing the best I could be doing. It's not like I flew across the hood of the car or got run over by the tires, I got knocked down.

I ended up skipping many classes and dropped my finance since there was no way I could keep up with it. I had found a new way to get around the house though— my desk chair. I sat in my chair, rolling it across the apartment, wishing I had thought of that weeks ago. By the time this injury was healed, I had spent hundreds of dollars on cab fares and the drivers knew me by name.

I decided it was time to just go for it and change my major to sociology but still pursue a minor in business. I also saw that there was the option for a concentration in critical animal studies, which I immediately felt compelled to take. I've always had a love for animals and feel a connection to them that I can't explain. I think this has to do with my social anxiety, which doesn't affect me at all when it comes to animals, only humans. Animals won't judge, they won't tell your secrets, and they will always be there to comfort you when you're sad.

I talked to an academic advisor and was told that I couldn't start taking sociology courses until the next school year, meaning for the rest of the term I could only register for electives such as philosophy. Basically, I couldn't get started on any sociology courses until I was in my third year of university.

I wasn't doing the best mentally; not because of the news from my academic advisor, but likely because of the season. During the summer my therapist had told me I have SAD, seasonal affective disorder, in which I become depressed in the fall and winter months when there is less sun. This made complete sense to me, but I didn't think of the implications it would have on my health living in a basement apartment.

Where my room was located, I only received a few hours of sunlight a day. The rest of the day was spent in artificial light, and when I was feeling depressed, I didn't even have those on. I often kept my blinds closed, not allowing the tiny bit of natural light to come in.

On my therapist's recommendation I got a therapy light that mimics sunlight and is extremely bright. I did my best to use this regularly, but I'm unsure if it ever helped or not. Either way, I know it didn't make anything worse. But I still wasn't doing well.

I resorted back to starving myself every once in a while as punishment for feeling depressed, but not nearly as much as I had in twelfth grade or first year of university. I was also feeling very self-conscious about the way I looked, even more so than normal. I was dealing with the same problems from high school, minus the braces and frizzy hair. This lack of confidence and overall social anxiety affected my grades, making it difficult to attend seminars in which I had to speak to earn marks. I had never had seminars in the past, only lectures where I could hide in the back and just listen.

My anxiety in social situations had always bothered me, but I finally decided to see Dr. Rodney about it because it was affecting my performance at school and in everyday life. He diagnosed me with social anxiety, which I didn't know existed. It made complete sense to me though, looking back on my life, both the early years and more recently in university.

Being in sociology was completely different for me. Even the homework was all different. Rather than doing projects and math, I was writing essays. This is what I preferred, but I was rusty and hadn't written an essay since high school. The marks I received were overall better than they had been since entering university, and this was able to boost my mood a bit.

—ℓℓ⁓

What didn't boost my mood was my phobia of spiders. As I had told my therapist years ago, this was one of my biggest fears, but it continued to worsen. Living in a basement apartment exacerbated my fear, as I was finding spiders and centipedes in the house every few days. Where did they come from? Thankfully I had housemates that were willing to kill them for me. Sometimes this wasn't an option, though.

As the warm water of a shower poured down on me one morning, I saw something weird in front of my face. With blurry and confused eyes I leaned closer, and discovered a spider hanging from a web on the shower head. I screamed, darted to the other end of the shower, grabbed my glasses from the counter, and threw water at the spider until it disappeared down the drain. I stood there shaking out of fright, breathing erratically, wondering if I could even finish my shower. Every few seconds I would twitch and check different areas of my skin, fearful that there was a spider on me. I decided to quickly finish washing up and ran like hell out of the bathroom into the safety of my room. Though I did find spiders in there sometimes, too. Ugh.

Another time, in the bathroom again, there was a large spider crawling on the floor. No one was home so I knew I had to get a cup to cover the spider so it wouldn't escape. I ran to the kitchen, breathing heavily with tears in my eyes, and grabbed a large glass. Holy crap, I don't know if I can do this. I have to though, if I lose sight of the spider I'll be even more terrified. I walked into the bathroom, the spider still in the same spot. I tried to control my breathing as it progressively got faster, beads of sweat forming on my face. My body began to tremble in terror. I can do this. I can do this. I can't do this. Shit, I have to do this.

These thoughts circled around my head for at least five minutes as I took steps toward and away from the spider, cup shaking in my hand. The spider made a move, and I knew I had to act quickly. I brought the glass down solidly onto the spider, jumped back, made sure it was trapped, and ran out of the room. My trembling got worse as I flew down the hallway into the kitchen, tears pouring from my eyes. I was so close to that spider, I almost touched it. I tried to calm down but every sound in the house made me jump. Every itch on my body made me twitch and shiver, paranoid it was a spider. After a housemate had killed it I still avoided stepping in that one spot, knowing a spider had touched it too.

At this point in my life I couldn't even say the word "spider." I called them "Ss." Seeing a picture of one made me recoil in fear, and videos were just ten times worse. Honestly, even seeing the word made me panic. I couldn't read it without cringing and I certainly couldn't type it. A housemate, Erin, made cupcakes with black liquorice legs for spiders, and I couldn't go near them.

Nowadays I'm still afraid of spiders, but not only can I type and say "spider," I can also kill small ones. Sometimes. Desperate times call for desperate measures. I still prefer not to look at photos of them and videos give me the chills before I have to turn my head. But this is much improved from before. The fear was debilitating at my worst points, causing constant trepidation.

———

When the summer rolled around I had a job which went well, though I missed a couple days for mental health reasons. I couldn't go to work if I couldn't stop crying. Before long, I was ready to head back to school. I was optimistic for a good year and excited to be back with my house-mates, us always having fun together.

Because of my depression I was always afraid to get drunk. My antidepressants specifically state on the containers not to consume alcohol while taking them, so I looked up online how true this really was.

I found that it affects everyone differently, but it's definitely possible for it to make you severely depressed for a few days after drinking. If I were to have suicidal thoughts for a few days after drinking that could be the end of me. There was no way I was going to risk getting depressed just to experience inebriation, so I didn't get drunk until my third year of university.

After moving back to school for the year, my friends and I were having a small party in our apartment and I decided that I was in a good enough headspace to try getting drunk. My friends knew of the risks and I made sure to let them know to check on me for the next few days in case there were any negative side effects.

I enjoyed myself and didn't limit how much I was drinking, eventually getting drunk. I was so drunk that I kept rolling off the couch. By the time the party was over I headed to my room, immediately vomiting all over my floor. Thank god there's tile in my room and not carpet. I'd have to clean that up tomorrow. Oh, and the splatters on the walls, too. And clean I did, grossed out with a shirt tied around my head to cover my nose and mouth, but feeling normal otherwise.

The next few days I remained myself, knowing now that it was safe for me to get drunk without becoming more depressed. I even found out I don't get hangovers. Nice.

Another time at home with my friends we decided to build a family on the Sims with all six of us. When it became time to create my character, I completed most of my face and body the way I wanted then moved to my nose. I didn't want to do this part but knew I had to. I stretched the sliders, making my nose as long and wide as I thought it was. When I showed the virtual me to my friends, I got an immediate "whoa!" from them.

"Why did you make your nose so big?" Melanie asked, laughing out of surprise at how ridiculous it appeared.

I honestly thought I had made it accurate. Melanie took control of the laptop and redid my nose, making it less than half the size I had it set to. She told me that what she did was realistic of what my nose looked like, and I saw that it really wasn't so bad. At least in her eyes it wasn't. I believed that she was telling the truth, that it may be the way others saw me, but I couldn't physically see it that way myself.

Ever since high school, the way I perceived my face varied from day to day, depending on my mood. If I was having a bad day or was depressed, my nose looked exponentially bigger and my acne more prominent. On a good day, my nose shrunk and my acne seemed faded. I never mentioned this to anyone, including professionals, even though it seemed to me like a sign of body dysmorphia. It was only that one part of my body that my mind altered.

Despite my beliefs, the changes Melanie made to my Sim helped me to see the distorted perceptions I carried with me; the way I view myself isn't the way others see me and my nose doesn't stand out as much as I think it does. It was still something I didn't like, but I could use this day to bolster my self-esteem by remembering how other people see me.

Even though I wasn't always in the best frame of mind, I loved living with my best friends and we had many fun times together. Each year we did a Secret Santa, and I got Melanie this specific year. I remembered her telling us, when she was drunk, that she liked to use shower heads with a hose because they were a great way to get off. For Christmas I bought her one of those shower heads. She was surprised, having forgotten that she had told us about her escapades. As Julia pointed out, it was the gift that keeps on giving.

—ℓ⁓

That wasn't the first time we had talked about our single sexual exploits to each other. I, for one, had a secret. Not among close friends or any of my housemates, but from everyone else in the world. While I had been feeling depressed for years, there were few things that could make me happy.

One of the things that did so was pleasuring myself. (Yes, I'm going there.) Almost everyone masturbates anyway, so it shouldn't be such a surprise that I do, too. By my second year of university, it had begun to get boring doing the same thing all the time. Living away from family, I was now free and comfortable to bring whatever I wanted into the house. Including toys. Or as I call them, friends.

I went online to search for high-quality vibrators to make my personal happy times happier, and I found myself in a world I didn't know existed. Seriously, there's stuff to electric shock people? And creepy animals with eyes you're supposed to put on yourself? No, thanks. Me being me, I did extensive research on materials, brands, noise levels, the ability to recharge, etcetera, and ended up with two classy toys I was happy with.

They did make me happier. So happy, in fact, that I ended up collecting friends. Currently I have ten toys, four of them vibrators. Whenever a human friend has questions about toys, they know who ask. They ask me, by the way, in case you weren't sure of the answer.

Back at my parents' place for the summer, Lindsay came home to visit. I was in my room on my laptop looking at sale items on an online sex shop, feeling sneaky that no one was the wiser. Now, when I say sale items, I'm talking about mostly cheaply made and often weird products. I was searching for a diamond in the rough. I didn't make it that far. I set my laptop down to go to the bathroom, screen open, sure no one would be going into my room in the next few minutes.

When I came back, lo and behold, there was Lindsay sitting on my bed with my laptop open. Seriously? My eyes widened in shock, unsure of what to do. I wracked my brain for something I could say to her to explain what I was doing or make a joke out of it—maybe just a "Haha, you caught me, some freaky stuff on there, eh?"

Ready to laugh it off with her and pretend to not be embarrassed, she said something to me completely unrelated to sex toys. What she said I can't remember, because my focus was on the fact that she looked so nonchalant. Okay, I guess we're pretending this never happened? That she didn't go on my laptop to see a giant, hairy jelly dildo among the items?

Well, well, well…This will make for an interesting discussion one day. I'm guessing that day will arrive when she reads this.

—ee—

That summer Lindsay got married and I was the maid of honour. I had planned and hosted her bridal shower a couple months beforehand, which all went well, but now it was time for me to write and say a speech to over one hundred people. Yikes. How do I write it so that everyone will be interested in what I'm saying? I need to make this speech good enough so that people will want to hear it and not get bored.

I wrote a three-minute speech, keeping it short and sweet, doing my best to only include things that people would like to hear but that also wouldn't embarrass Lindsay and her husband, Matt. I decided I would read it, so that relieved some of my nerves.

During the reception, when it was my turn to speak, I prefaced my speech by saying that it would be short and not nearly as funny as the other speeches they'd hear that night. As I spoke, I saw that everyone had their eyes on me, meaning I was at least holding their attention, but I also noticed that they were laughing at my jokes. A lot.

I got a loud round of applause at the end and many congratulations later on for my great speech. Wow. I had been too critical of myself, assuming people would find my words boring. They weren't though. I needed to have more faith in myself. Not just in my words, but in everything I do.

In my fourth year of university, things went downhill. While most of my friends were ready to graduate, I was in limbo. The year began with a sense of excitement and hope just as the others had, but it quickly deteriorated. I had attended a couple lectures and seminars, both of them making me nervous.

Often when I'm nervous—and this has happened for as long as I can remember—I get diarrhea. I'd have to factor that in to the time it took me to get ready for school and knowing I'd likely get it made me more anxious. In addition to this, I get very sweaty when nervous. It became more prominent when going on antidepressants, sweat frequently covering my whole body. It made me feel disgusting, dirty, but most of all embarrassed. What was wrong with me? Why do I get hot so easily? It's like I'm a sweaty man and I hate it.

My thoughts ran wild in lectures thinking of all the things I did wrong and ways I looked wrong. It felt as if there were a spotlight on me and everyone was judging what I was doing. Could the professor sense the fear in my eyes among these hundred people? Did students think I was sitting awkwardly? Is my face red? Are they repulsed by my acne that's flaring up? Did they know that I'm freaking out inside? I wish it were cooler in here, how can people have sweaters on?

Seminars were worse. There were fewer than twenty people in each seminar so I felt even more on display. How could I talk to get participation marks when I could barely enter the room? Do they see how much I'm sweating from nerves? Oh god of course they see me sweating but that makes me even hotter. Shit, I need to control my breathing, that's getting worse too.

Keep breathing, you don't want to hyperventilate or have a panic attack in front of these people. That would be even more embarrassing than you're already making yourself to be.

Why did I even bother coming to the seminar if I'm not going to talk? I shouldn't be here, I'm wasting everyone's time. I'm so ugly anyway that they would be happier if I wasn't in class. I shouldn't subject people to having to look at me. I don't even want to look at me. I probably gross people out with how much acne I have, and I don't blame them. It is disgusting, and I am disgusting.

The act alone of even walking throughout the school had me panicked. Am I walking weird or normal? I don't even know how to walk properly, apparently. Where should I put my hands? I guess let them fall to my side, but it would be easier if I had a drink in my hand. And that would keep me cooler. Where are my eyes supposed to go? I should stick to looking down at the floor and up only sometimes. I don't want to catch anyone's eye by mistake. They'd wonder why I was staring at them. Why are so many people looking at me? Seriously, is my face that red and sweaty? Let's walk faster. I've got to get out of here. This isn't normal. I'm not normal.

I forced myself to make an appointment with a therapist on campus to maybe help me with my anxiety, and in the first session I burst out crying. I told her about all the struggles I was having and that I felt suicidal that day. Once my crying was under control she took me across campus to see the mental health nurse. As we walked through the halls it felt like even more people were staring at me than normal, probably seeing my watery, pink, sad eyes.

In the mental health nurse's office, the nurse sat me down with a juice to help calm me. I told her the problems I was having and she gave me a number to call if I felt I was a danger to myself. It was a service where a mental health professional and police officer would come to my door, assess me, and take me to the hospital if needed. She also got me an appointment with a doctor on campus who excelled in the area of mental health.

The doctor I saw put me on a new medication in addition to the others I was already on. She provided me with many doctor's notes which I could give to my professors to have my assignments extended, but I didn't end up using any of them. I was too afraid to hand in the papers and soon this fear prevented me from going to anymore classes at all. I also never saw the on-campus therapist again, too frightened to return, even though I told my parents I was still seeing her.

I stopped doing everything. In fact, my fears stopped me from leaving the house most of the time. I spent nearly every day hidden in my room. Did I have agoraphobia? Leaving the house was a terrifying thought, and physically doing it was something I could rarely handle. I wasn't afraid of the outside world though, it was the people out there whom I feared. If I left the house someone could see me. They would notice how scared I looked. My acne would bring even more attention to myself. What if I started crying or had a panic attack? I couldn't risk it. Going outside was too dangerous. Home was my safe place.

My lowest point of social anxiety was when I couldn't go to the grocery store to buy toilet paper. Every day for a week I would try to push myself to go to the store, failing each time and crumbling into a ball of tears. Failure.

You are a failure. Glad you see that. You can't even buy toilet paper. Pathetic.

When there was one roll left I forced myself to walk up to Melanie and asked her in shame if she could buy toilet paper for me. She said of course and I handed her a ten dollar bill, slowly walking back to my room, shoulders hunched in defeat. I can't believe I couldn't do it. I couldn't fucking buy toilet paper. Forget that, I can believe it.

You're afraid of everything so why would this be any different? Good luck living the rest of your life like this. God, you're worthless. Seriously, how much more pitiful can you get than not leaving the house for toilet paper? Yeah, I thought so. Just stay in your room, it's where you belong.

Days and nights blended into each other, little light in my room to tell the difference. It became regular for me to go to sleep at three in the morning and wake up in the early afternoon. That way I could be awake when other people were at school or sleeping.

One morning I woke up at nine. Except it wasn't morning, it was night. I had slept from three in the morning until nine at night, thoroughly confused. I was surprised at first how dark it was in my room seeing as the clock said nine, but then I saw that it was actually p.m. and not a.m. How had I slept so long? Oh well, it's not like I was doing much else.

Moving home to my parents' house late that spring was difficult. Most of my friends had graduated while I had dropped out. I was used to living with my best friends for four years, and now I didn't know if I'd ever see them again. I'm not the best at keeping in touch with people, which causes guilt, just as it did when I was a child. It was especially difficult at this point, when my social anxiety was so debilitating. What made things easier was knowing I was going on vacation soon.

That summer my parents, Nicole, and I went on a Caribbean cruise. This was our second cruise together, the first one being several years earlier. In early grade twelve, when my mom first brought up the idea of going on a cruise, I was very hesitant. Yes, it sounded like fun to go on vacation in about half a year's time, but I was almost positive I'd be dead by then. I told her I was afraid of being on the water for so long, which was true, but I also didn't want to waste my parents' money. If they purchased tickets for me to go on a cruise with them and I was most likely to kill myself before we left, I'd be more of a disappointment than I already felt I was.

This time around things were different. I was struggling with my social anxiety but was determined to not let it get in the way. And I wasn't having any suicidal thoughts. Nicole and I planned on surfing and parasailing, and I almost went zip-lining but I chickened out. The surfing and parasailing were still way out of my comfort zone so my parents were pretty impressed I was willing to try them.

Getting ready for a day of surfing at Cocoa Beach in Florida, I slathered on a buttload of sunscreen and grabbed my cover up, hat, and shades. I could never be too careful, I burn easily. As we walked on the hot, soft sand toward the surfboards, my feet burned. Really burned. I ended up running awkwardly until I made it onto one of the surfboards. Who wants burned feet on vacation? I took off my sun gear and put on a surf shirt, glad my shoulders would still be covered. We were given a short demonstration on what to do and I was already struggling to follow on land.

We took our boards to the water and paddled as we had been instructed to do, pushing past the current of the ocean. The cool water was such a relief from the sun beating down on us. With an instructor by my side, I learned how to catch a wave.

The first time I forgot to stand up, and kept lying on my stomach and feeling as if I were on a water slide. The next ten, twenty, thirty, probably forty times I tried standing up and the most I could do was get one knee lifted up. Every time I crashed into the water I got a mouthful of saltwater and it stung my eyes too. Though I did feel self-conscious about falling off so often, it was helped by not being able to see anyone properly. I wasn't wearing glasses or contacts. We continued surfing for a whole two hours in the heat of the afternoon sun.

When we swam back to shore my family noticed how pink I was. I said I was fine, knowing how much lotion I had put on earlier, not realizing that the ocean had washed it all off, plus having all the water reflecting the sun onto me for hours. For the next few hours we stayed indoors as much as possible, my face beginning to feel tighter and hotter.

When we arrived at our room on the ship I looked in the mirror and saw a deep red colour to my face. And blisters. All over and around my nose and forehead. There was water, or some sort of fluid, underneath my skin. I was mortified, wondering how I could be seen in public looking like this. Mom gave me aloe vera to soothe my skin and I carefully applied it before bed.

The next morning my parents stared at me in shock and Nicole screamed. They then began laughing at my face as I stared back with tired eyes. What now? I walked to the bathroom and looked at my reflection in the mirror. Was that me? I was almost unrecognizable. My family really was laughing at my face. It had swelled from the aloe vera, an allergic reaction I was not expecting. You could barely see my eyes they were so swollen. I started laughing and crying at the same time, unable to process what was happening. My mom wanted to say it wasn't as bad as it seemed, but it really was that bad. Nicole begged to take a picture but I refused.

Looking back on it all, I wish she had just taken a picture. It really was as bad as it sounds, worse even. In fact, my sister says that was the best day of her life. Just the mention of this story sends her into a laughing fit.

I was too scared to face the outside world and stayed in the room the rest of the day, my parents bringing me food. What if it stays like this the rest of the trip? What about all the activities we had planned, and the places I wanted to go? What if when the swelling eventually goes down I get scars from the blisters that were still on my face?

The next day my face was slightly less swollen, the most noticeably puffy part being my eyes. My parents convinced me to leave our room and come with them around the ship but I was terrified. What will people think of me? I conceded, but on one condition: I wanted to wear my sunglasses and a hat all day. It was awkward going to a live show at night in the theatre with my sunglasses and hat on, but I knew that made me more comfortable than going without them.

The day after that I tried going out with nothing covering my face but kept my face tilted down. I think and care way too much about what others think of me. My whole life I've spent worrying about the reactions other people could have to things I did or the way I looked, instead of just doing things for me. What difference would it have made if people saw my face in all its swollen, blistered glory? People may have stared or felt sorry for me, but that wouldn't change who I was, and didn't need to change how I felt about myself.

CHAPTER SEVEN

ROAD TO RECOVERY

AFTER OUR VACATION I promptly began seeing an occupational therapist named Theresa. We got along well and worked on various things such as trying to get to the roots of my negative thoughts. I was currently unemployed and wasn't in school, so I felt as if I was going nowhere in life. I was a failure and had a bleak future, if any.

Another thing we worked on was to try and get me out of my comfort zone socially. One of my tasks was to walk around the block. That got axed pretty quickly though because what would people think if they saw me randomly walking down the street? It was too risky.

Something I could try though, was walking my dog, Sophie. My new task was to walk around the block with her a couple times a week. I tried it once but was terrified and didn't go back out. What if a neighbour came outside and saw me? What if they wondered why I was back home? What if someone tried to talk to me? All the possibilities were too much to handle.

Theresa soon suggested I consider participating in a group therapy program for people with social anxiety. I immediately went into panic mode, tears and fear in my eyes, breathing heavily, and telling her no. No, no, no. Way too scary. How can you expect someone terrified of people to talk to a group of strangers about how they scare her? Would anyone else even show up? If we all have social anxiety, I can't see many people attending. I told her I would consider it in the future, but as of now, it was too much.

As well as Theresa, I also saw a psychiatrist. She too helped me work out my thoughts and was the one in charge of my medication. She prescribed me a medicine that was usually for those with psychosis, but I was given a much smaller dose. This was to help with my rapid thoughts that quickly spiraled into self-hate. Going on that medication was different than any other I had been on. Though it only took me a bit over a week to adjust, it was a weird week.

The first day I had to spend in bed. My head felt so heavy, tight and drugged that I could barely walk. Even though using the computer made me dizzier, I started searching to find out if my brain was swelling. Maybe that's what this feeling was? Just going to the bathroom was a struggle because I couldn't walk straight.

I considered contacting the psychiatrist but already knew that medications can have an adjustment period, so I hung in there and hoped what I was feeling was at least somewhat normal. From what I read online I wasn't in serious danger, so I'd put my trust in Google. Don't let me down. In the following days my symptoms thankfully decreased, but I began feeling high from the medication.

I would giggle and laugh for no reason, and was having difficulty controlling my emotions. At Dairy Queen that week with my mom and Nicole, we were waiting in line and I was talking a bit too loud about how drugged up I felt. Then I began giggling and was embarrassed that I couldn't stop. Fortunately this didn't last much longer and I felt normal enough on the medicine thereafter.

Another thing I tried, much different from medication, was meditation and mindfulness. I tried many different types, always finding that my thoughts would get in the way. The meditations would tell me to just let the thoughts pass through, but how can I do that when they're just circling around my head? There were two things that were able to keep the thoughts at bay. One was progressive muscle relaxation and the other was meditation through music.

For progressive muscle relaxation I lie down at night under the covers in my bed with earphones in, listening to a meditation guide me through the steps. I curl my toes tightly to tense them for a few seconds, then release, letting them feel lighter yet heavy at the same time, sinking into the bed. Next are my feet as a whole—tense and release. Calves, thighs, butt, all the way up to the top of my head. I even throw a Kegel in there every now and then.

With my mind focused on tensing and releasing my muscles, there aren't negative thoughts floating around in my head. I continue to lie on my bed for a few minutes just to enjoy the feelings of being at peace and relaxed, a slight smile on my face. I know I need to take the earphones out before falling asleep, slightly breaking me out of my trance. But I also know that within a few short minutes I'll be in a deep sleep.

While meditating through music I listen to instrumental songs by artists such as Lights & Motion, whom I adore. I've always had such a huge love for music that I have an excellent pair of headphones with great sound to make the experience even better.

With this type of meditation I sit down so I'm in a comfortable position with my eyes closed, no one around me. I play the music, listening for each instrument. What can I find? Drums, guitar, bass, violin, piano, synthesizers, and more. I follow how the music flows, as it picks up speed and slows down again. Where are the instruments? I can hear them surrounding my whole head, several closer and others farther away. Some parts of the song or instrument are only on one side, while others circle around me. What feelings does this song provoke? There are no words in almost all this artist's songs, but you can feel the passion, hope, intensity, and every other emotion surging through him.

It captivates me. There is no room for negative thoughts, or thoughts of any kind. None other than this glorious music that moves me to my core. It can make me feel so powerful, bring tears to my eyes in sadness or happiness, and just feel *everything*. I can't describe how liberating this form of meditation is for me. It just *is*.

If you want to let go, get away from everything, try this. It takes you to another place. Far away in my mind yet still here in my body. I don't feel headphones covering my ears, I am one with the music. This is something that I will continue to do on a regular basis as it's so cathartic. Even if it doesn't work for you, there's nothing to lose.

After six months of seeing Theresa and the psychiatrist I decided that I was ready for group therapy. The idea of it no longer made me tear up or freak out, just very nervous. I signed up for a social anxiety program with CAMH, the Centre for Addiction and Mental Health, with a focus on CBT. This program was three months long and I would attend once a week.

Getting to my first class was easy enough. I was already familiar with downtown Toronto from previous summer jobs. I was full of nerves and the same thoughts came up that did when I first heard about the program. Are people even going to show up to a social anxiety program? Is this something I'm strong enough to handle? Walking into the building, I took the elevator and headed straight to the bathroom to calm and cool myself down.

You can do this. You got this far already and other people are just as nervous. You have a few minutes to just relax in here, but then you have to go in. It's for the best, trust me.

I left the bathroom and walked into the meeting room, greeted by friendly faces and welcomes. There were about eight other people in this class, each with their own experiences and versions of social anxiety.

To begin the program we wrote down our core belief and what evidence we had to prove it. My core belief was that I was a failure and I was convinced of this with ninety-nine percent of my being. I easily filled up a page of experiences that led to this way of thinking, from my early childhood to dropping out of school. These experiences caused me to hold onto blame and guilt, feel as if I wasn't good enough, taught me to stay hidden away from my problems, and led me to believe that if I don't do something right then I'm a failure.

We reframed these thoughts, which was much more difficult than I anticipated, and created a new core belief to aspire to. Mine was that I have had success in my life. It was originally that I am successful, but that was too unrealistic to achieve in my mind. Even with the easier to attain belief, I still only perceived it as one percent true. Putting together a list of experiences to validate my new core belief was incredibly difficult and I couldn't even fill up all the available space we were given.

Next, we wrote out what made us anxious on a scale from zero to one-hundred. My zero was being with family and very close friends, while one-hundred was going on a date or to a party without a safety person. We had to start facing our fears, preferably starting anywhere from thirty to fifty, to push ourselves out of our comfort zones yet not cause panic attacks. I decided to start with asking a stranger for directions, a twenty-five on my scale. I was able to do so that week and was proud of myself, but felt that I could push myself farther.

Since buying things scared me, a couple times during this program I tried talking to a cashier as I was checking out, but each time I worried about making a fool out of myself and having them see me as stupid and awkward. The first time I talked to a cashier I made a comment about how cold it was outside, and he said he thought it was warm. Fail. My anxiety only increased as did my belief in my stupidity.

I tried again soon after at another store, Tim Hortons, asking how long their Valentine's Day doughnut would be available. The cashier was unsure and asked another employee, both of them baffled as to the answer. Fail. Again my anxiety increased, and I regretted saying anything in the first place. As I walked out I forgot to take the hot chocolate I had ordered. I was too stupid to even remember a friggin' hot chocolate.

Still determined to do well in the social anxiety program, I went out more in general, tagging along with my mom and Nicole on some of their many shopping trips. Sometimes while in the mall I'd have to sit outside of a store to cool off, giving myself some space from the crowds of people in each aisle.

While in one store I recognized Joseph, my childhood best friend. It had been almost ten years since I last saw him. I wanted to say hello but was afraid: What if it isn't him, then I'll look like an idiot. What if he doesn't recognize me? He'll see how sweaty and ugly I am, including how big my nose is. He won't want to see me anyway. I began panicking, unsure if this was something I could do. My breathing increased, my tense body overheated and my eyes watered. Oh, no, I have to get away or I'll hyperventilate.

After this barrage of negative thoughts, I did my best not to be noticed by him. I wanted to get out of the store without him seeing me, but at the same time I still wanted to push myself to talk to him. I worked up the courage to get his attention and say hello, asking how he was doing. He did recognize me and looked happy to see me, making my fears invalid.

Each week of the program we would fill out sheets that explained situations that made us nervous, how much of each emotion we were feeling, thoughts that went through our heads, how anxious we got, and what evidence we had to prove our thoughts right or wrong.

Every time I filled out a sheet my negative thoughts were proved wrong and it was very eye opening to see how common it was for me to think poorly of myself. I already knew it was bad, but reading it out loud to others in the group really got me thinking. Would I ever think these things about someone else? Never. I was becoming aware of just how distorted my thoughts really were.

This program was changing much more than just my fear of people. It was altering my entire outlook on life. My depression and social anxiety were so closely related that they would often blend into each other. They were both fueled by my negative thoughts. Always spiraling me into the depths of despair. I needed this program to finally get me out of this purgatory I was stuck in. To change the years of built up negative thoughts that were the crutch I leaned upon. To tear down the wall I had built up that kept me from living my life. I was creating a new me. A more confident, happy, content me.

I think working in a group environment helped a lot more than talking one-on-one with Theresa because it forced me to do more work. I felt it was necessary to complete the homework each week in group therapy so that others couldn't judge me if I didn't get it done. That may not be the best way to encourage me to complete the homework, and I most definitely did want to push myself too, but at least I had found ways to do it. If I didn't regularly fill out the worksheets each week, I wouldn't have been able to learn so much about myself. I'm also glad I made it to almost every class.

Some of the tasks we had during our sessions were difficult, while others were extremely nerve wracking. One thing we had to do was hold a five-minute one-on-one conversation with someone. That was one of the very high situations on my scale that made me nervous.

I don't know how to hold conversations. Period. My mind goes blank, other than the negative thoughts in my head. All I can think about is what am I supposed to say, how I can get out of this situation, and how stupid and awkward do I look right now. I have trouble meeting the person's eyes, afraid that they will see right through me to all my fears. Even if the other person starts the conversation with a typical "hey, how are you?" my response is usually "good." That's it. I don't remember to add the "and you?" Such simple social skills eluded me.

Each of these classes left me exhausted, yet I knew it was worth it.

One day we were told that we would be filmed doing something on camera. We could do anything from reading a book out loud to dancing. The first time I went on camera I decided to do charades and felt very nervous. There was a point when I paused for at least fifteen seconds (I know this because we had to watch our videos afterwards). We gave each other feedback and it wasn't as embarrassing as I thought it would be.

Weeks later we had to be on video again, and this time I chose to dance to Nelly's "Hot in Herre." I had done this before to cheer up close friends, but never in front of people I didn't know well. I did feel a level of comfort around this group of people though, and so I was going to go all out.

On the day of the dance I arrived with my jacket done up. I set my iPad on the table with the lyrics on the screen, played the song, and began singing. Well, rapping. I let myself move to the music and just have fun, pretending I was doing karaoke. As it got to the chorus, I started stripping and took my jacket off. The next time the chorus came around I took off a sweater. Next, unbutton my blouse—I still had a shirt on underneath. Not wanting to flash anyone, I moved to my boots. Before I knew it, the song had ended, and I was so proud of myself.

I got a huge applause and the other members of the group told me how brave I was. Some of them said they wouldn't have been able to do what I did. It meant a lot to me because I wouldn't have been able to do that before, either, and they were all supportive. When I had to watch it with everyone else afterwards, I felt even more proud. I had fun, so there was less self-judgement.

During the last couple weeks of the program I became depressed. It was odd because it was spring, and if anything I should be coming out of a depression at that time. When going to my sessions my demeanour was different. Much less optimistic. I told them that I had been feeling depressed. I pushed myself less for my weekly homework of exposing myself to my fears, no longer showing much progress.

When the final class arrived, I woke up feeling even more depressed. I was a failure. I had achieved so much in this program and the last couple weeks I failed. Why bother going to the final class? I don't deserve it. I wish I'd just die. I decided not to go to the final class. I couldn't have anyone see how low I'd fallen, plus this was a good way to punish myself.

My parents found out that I hadn't gone, and I felt even more disappointed in myself. That night I lay on my bed crying, wishing I wasn't here anymore. All that progress put to shit. I'd be happier if I just died.

Nicole came into my room to talk to me, asking how I was feeling. My family knew by now to straight up ask me if I was having suicidal thoughts, even though I hadn't had them in at least a year. I told her yes, I was feeling suicidal, but it wasn't serious. I wasn't close to where I was other times. She told my parents and they all agreed I should go to the emergency room. I didn't agree. Why bother wasting everyone's time? I wasn't about to kill myself so there was no emergency. I eventually gave in to please them and we all drove to the hospital together.

After a couple hours in the crowded waiting room my thoughts had calmed down, but I couldn't get out that easily. I sure wanted out though, I hate the smell of hospitals and I don't know if it's true or not but I just feel like I'm collecting germs and diseases in there.

I was called to another area and talked to multiple nurses and doctors, telling them that though I was feeling suicidal before, I wasn't going to hurt myself. They made me promise, and I did. I meant it. An appointment was set up to see a well-respected doctor in two weeks at the hospital to go over my medication and see how I was feeling.

In those two weeks before the appointment I didn't feel well, but I wasn't suicidal. I went to my appointment feeling depressed, unsure of how things would go. The doctor decided to switch one of the medications I was on with another, and I agreed. Why not? I was to take it in the morning, along with another pill I was already on, because he felt they would be more effective taken at that time of day. He also referred me to a different therapist and psychiatrist than the ones I was previously seeing, and I agreed to that change as well.

The next two weeks my mood improved. Greatly. My parents noticed a difference within a few days, I noticed within a week. Things felt different. Really different. It was hard to comprehend, but I felt happy. Genuinely happy. I didn't know if it was the medicine, the fact that it was the summer, if it was the CAMH program, or a combination of everything. I saw the doctor again and told him all this, and his response was that it was probably many different factors. No matter what the true answer was, we were both pleased.

Something in me just felt free. All of me felt free. Free from my mind. From the negative thoughts that consumed me, the depressive cloud over my head, and a constant fear of people. I was smiling more, feeling optimistic, and even wanted to go back to school. I didn't have the money, but having that desire cross my mind more than once was a great sign of my mental health.

When I told my parents that I was thinking about going back to school at some point, they offered to pay for it. Holy crap, are they serious? I immediately started crying, feeling so grateful. Because of the way I was feeling and the progress I had made in the social anxiety program, I decided to take a huge leap and go to school that fall, just in a couple months.

Within a week of making this decision I had found a house to rent with five other students, saw the house, and signed the lease. My bedroom was on the first floor with two windows and I confirmed with the landlord that it received lots of sunlight. It most definitely did. I was going to live with five strangers. Wow, had I ever improved. I registered for my courses and was ready. I was heading back into this not knowing anyone, all my friends having graduated. Could I really do this? Yes, I could.

Back at home everything was going well, but I was terrified my depression would come back once school started. My therapist and I created a sheet that I could keep with me all the time to help my mental health. It was a chart of triggers, interventions, and people to call.

Before I knew it school had started, and I had that chart taped on the wall beside my bed. I read it each morning and night, smiling each time because I wasn't being triggered, I didn't need the interventions, and I didn't have to call anyone for mental health reasons.

CHAPTER EIGHT

STARTING OVER

JUST BECAUSE I wasn't depressed and had taken that social anxiety program didn't mean I was completely healed. I was still socially anxious, but I could now go to school, both lectures and seminars. I took a more manageable course load, three or four courses per semester rather than five so I wouldn't become too stressed. I was fearful of taking a full course load. Would it lead me to become depressed again? Have suicidal thoughts? I couldn't risk that.

When I had PMS I still became emotional and easily irritated, but to a much lesser extent. There were valid reasons for the crying and anger, to a point. If I felt that my emotions were getting too extreme I would talk to a doctor about my birth control and get it changed, but otherwise it wasn't too big of a deal for me.

I went out every couple weeks to get groceries and it still scared me, but I did it. I got along with my new housemates, though I spent most of my time in my room doing school work.

Homework was still scary for me. I was afraid it would trigger the depression. I took things slowly and realized that it wasn't making my thoughts spiral into a depression. I remained levelheaded, got things done, and was able to concentrate. If I got too stressed or frustrated I'd make a tea. Both the act of making it and drinking it I found soothing. I had to teach myself that homework did not equal suicidal thoughts. I didn't make any close friends, but that wasn't one of my goals. I wanted to be at school and *go* to school. One step at a time.

A step I did want to try to take was into the dating world. I had never been on a date before, scaling it at one hundred on my list of fears for a reason. It was the ultimate one-on-one conversation. A planned talk with no immediate escape and the other party knowing I'm interested in them. Being aware that they too are interested in me, but that their feelings could change at any second. It was fear of the unknown.

Not only was the idea of dating terrifying to me, I didn't want to be with anyone when I wasn't healthy. I believed that in order to have someone else love me, I had to love myself first. That was a long road. When I was still depressed and very socially anxious I thought that if anyone tried to date me they would regret it. In my mind I had nothing to give and they would find out quickly I wasn't worth it.

In first year university there was a guy I'm pretty sure was interested in me after working on a project together and he even hinted a couple times that I should go out with him to the local bar. I liked him too, but was fearful and knew I couldn't be with him when I hated myself. I chose to avoid him for the rest of the year, walking in the other direction if I ever accidentally caught his eye. Anyone else I ever suspected of possibly wanting more than just friendship I'd ignore and stay away from too. It's what I'd done my whole life.

Now that I was ready for this new adventure, how should I start? I'm not exactly the kind of person who can just walk up to people, so I decided to try online dating and joined eHarmony. I got along well for a few weeks with one guy I met online and decided to meet him in person. Wow, my first date; at twenty-three. Just a bit of a late bloomer, right?

The day of my date arrived quickly. As I walked up to meet him he looked exactly as he did in his photos. This was a good sign—he probably was real and not there to kill me. We walked into a café and got drinks, chatting about random topics, including subjects we had talked about online and over texts. Underneath the table my legs were shaking, but apparently he couldn't tell. I had asked him if he noticed.

The date was going really well and I couldn't have asked for more, other than a spark. It just felt like we were friends and so I had to tell him that I didn't think we were right for each other. I felt horrible for doing that, but I didn't want to lead him on.

Shortly after, I met another guy online and before I knew it I was on my second date ever. He wasn't a killer, either. This date had a better feel to it and we decided to see each other again. We went out for about two months until he called things off, though we were only ever dating. Although I felt devastated at the time, I was also happy he ended it because I knew he wasn't right for me. It was time I get more involved with school to take my mind off guys, meet new people, and have more of a presence on campus.

My parents and my closest friend from high school, Melissa, had been encouraging me to join a club or do something to get involved on campus since the beginning of that school year. Actually, my parents had been telling me that since the beginning of high school. As for Melissa, she thought I might meet a cute guy there.

I was ready now, so I searched Brock's website to see what clubs there were. I considered joining the animal rights club, but their website stated as a baseline they preferred people to be vegans, and I was only a vegetarian. That scared me off.

As I continued my search, I stumbled across a club called Active Minds. They were dedicated to raising mental health awareness and stomping the stigma associated with mental health and illness. *This is where I fit*, I thought.

I contacted the President of the club and she let me know where and when they were meeting next. The fear was real, but so was the excitement. I'm going to do everything I can to be an active member; I don't want to sit in the background. If I'm committing myself to this, I'm going all the way.

The day of the first meeting arrived and I slowly walked into the room, asking if this was the meeting for Active Minds. Of course it was, I had checked the room and date a million times. Oh, god, I'm really doing this. There's no turning back.

You can do it, just be yourself.

The President told me I was in the right place and I was greeted with a warm welcome from everyone. I participated a lot in that meeting, sharing ideas and agreeing to help promote a concert the next day. I was terrified to promote this event because it meant I had to do tabling. Tabling involved standing by a table and interacting with students, letting them know about the club. In this case, I was convincing them to go to the concert. Despite the fear, I could do it. I just had to do my best to stay calm.

Something else that was brought up during the meeting was that they were looking for student speakers to talk at an open community event. There would be four speakers sharing their experience with mental health and I wanted to be one of those people. As scared as it made me, it was the right step to take.

Another thing that made me nervous was the cute guy sitting beside me at the club meeting. He had the most extraordinary blue eyes. I instantly had a crush on him and after the meeting he walked me to my bus stop. We had kept a conversation going the whole time, he was quite easy to talk to. It wasn't too often I found people like that. Today was a pretty good day.

Tabling the next day wasn't as scary as I thought it would be. It helped having a couple other Active Minds members there to do it with me, so I didn't feel like I had to step too far out of my comfort zone. The guy with the blue eyes, Brett, was supposed to be tabling at that same time but was sick. Damn it. I'll just keep trying to table at the same times as him.

The next time I tabled it was for Eating Disorders Awareness Week. I held a white board that had written on it: You're beautiful (and handsome) inside and out. I spent hours throughout the week holding up that sign, feeling like I was making a difference. I got countless students and staff saying thank you with bright smiles as they walked by and read the sign, and even a fair number of "you too."

As early as a year ago I would've assumed people were just being polite or saying "you too" so I didn't have to feel as ugly as I really was. But this isn't how I interpreted their words. I accepted what they were saying at face value, believing that I was pretty too. One guy even gave me his number and after a few days of hesitation I texted him only to find out he was looking for someone just to hook-up with. That was so not me. Delete.

Since Active Minds was looking for speakers for the upcoming mental health night, I decided to send in a speech I had drafted. Writing this speech was cathartic because it showed how much improvement I had made in a short time. The speech was accepted and I was chosen to be one of the four speakers! I was full of excitement and nerves, wanting to do this so badly yet worrying I may mess up. I could do this. I can do this. Just because I had messed up when I was younger didn't mean it would happen again. Besides, I could read this whole speech.

A couple weeks later I was tabling alone. I was too scared to call people over so I let them come to me instead. One woman who did walk toward me began going off on a tangent. I didn't agree with a fair bit of what she said, making me unsure of what I should be saying to her. She talked while I mostly just listened for twenty minutes.

There are times when I begin to feel more comfortable in a one-on-one conversation but this was not one of those situations. As the minutes wore on I became more and more nervous, heating up and feeling trapped. I pretended to act normal but inside I was freaking out.

Brett then appeared, not even signed up to table with me, and saw that I was uncomfortable. He stepped up to help me out, taking hold of the conversation until the woman left. As soon as she was out of sight I thanked Brett, my eyes beginning to water. I was overheated and felt so uncomfortable that I was worried I may have a panic attack. I did my best to regulate my breathing that was speeding up while controlling my tears. As I calmed down I thanked him again. He didn't realize just how much he had helped. Or how I just wanted to hug and kiss him, but not yet.

Be patient Michelle, he may ask you out, he seems to be interested.

I ended my tabling duties early because of that situation, and Brett asked if I'd like to have a chat soon since we could both relate to having anxiety, though in different ways. We were also both going to speak at the mental health night. I agreed. I felt comfortable around him.

Before meeting up with Brett for our chat, I wondered what it really was. A date? A therapy session? I was reading too far into things and had to relax. I was nervous when I saw him at first, but those nerves went away soon after. We ended up talking for over three hours. That's a lot for me. With anyone.

It was so much more than I was used to that I lost my voice when I got home. I could barely get any words out and this wouldn't have been much of a problem for me if it weren't for the mental health night being the next day. Shoot. Would my voice be back in time? I didn't want to cancel; I refused to cancel.

The next morning my voice came back a bit. It was still in rough shape, but you could hear me now. By midday it slightly improved, and by the evening (when the event was to take place) my voice was halfway to normal. Now I had extra nerves for my speech. What would people think of my voice? What if they thought that's how I always sounded? I decided to make a note of it at the beginning of my speech, saying that I apologized for my voice not being normal. Though this wasn't necessary to do at all, it gave me a sense of comfort.

My speech went well, better than I could have expected. It wasn't memorized at all so I just had to read from papers, but for me to share the content was nerve-racking. Telling people I had lived with depression and social anxiety, that I had almost tried to kill myself, was one of the scariest yet most rewarding experiences of my life.

Later that night I was talking to Brett over Facebook when he asked me out. He said he couldn't wait any longer and apologized for not doing it in person, but there was no need for an apology. This was a damn good day.

Our first date went as well as it could have possibly gone. Since we were students, we took the bus to a restaurant. Yes, I felt a bit awkward and fairly nervous, but aren't those things normal to feel on a first date? I really impressed him with my order. A veggie burger and a pitcher of beer for us to share. I had a craving for a burger and beer, so why not? If he thought my choices weren't lady-like enough that would be his loss, not mine. He ended up ordering a burger as well and we spent our whole dinner talking and laughing.

We headed back to his apartment afterward to hang out and we continued to talk about everything. We were having deep conversations, not just surface level, and it was so refreshing. I stayed overnight as the busses had stopped running by the time we thought to look at the clock.

While falling asleep feeling relaxed, I let out a fart. Ugh, why does this always happen to me? At least this was more of a cute toot than anything major. We burst out laughing, my face turning red as I buried it into the pillow, feeling embarrassed but not overly so. Once our giggling had quieted we fell asleep, snuggled warmly in the bed. I knew I was going to fall in love with this man.

As a result of my speaking at the mental health night, I was asked to share my story in a couple weeks on film for Brock's new mental health website. I immediately agreed, wanting to share my story with as many people as possible.

The day of filming arrived before I knew it and the nerves hit again. I knew I could do this though. All I had to do was read my speech on a teleprompter and answer a few questions at the end. While answering the questions I became nervous. I did my best with my responses unsure if it was what they were looking for. When the video was put online they had cut out the whole speech and left just my answers to their questions. I looked terrified. It was true—I was. I left the video up because I have to believe that even though I look scared in that video, others will see strength and that they too can speak out about their experience with mental illness.

—ℓℓ—

Although I felt much more confident about myself at this time, there was still something that was bothering me. My nose. I had always wanted to change my nose but was never in the right frame of mind to make a rational decision. I was finally in the right frame of mind. I was no longer depressed, my social anxiety was under control, overall I was happy with how I looked, my nose just did not fit. With my petite frame and shy demeanour, a large nose did not suit my size or personality. I knew that getting rhinoplasty was the right decision because I wanted to do this for myself, not for others. It was a decision I didn't take lightly and made sure to do plenty of research.

I first went to an ENT (ear nose throat) doctor for a deviated septum because I also had trouble breathing through my nose my whole life, and eventually was referred to a plastic surgeon who would fix my deviated septum and reconstruct my nose. It was like a dream come true, knowing I was finally going to have my facial features balanced out. I was told by the surgeon that the surgery was about improvement and not perfection, and I was in complete agreement. I then booked my surgery, only a month from that time.

When the day of the surgery arrived, I sat tense in the car as my dad drove me to the hospital. It felt like I had been waiting for this day since forever, yet it came so quickly at the same time.

I walked into the hospital, got registered, and was taken to a room where I had to change into the typical hospital gown that exposes your butt. I shut that thing tight. The most terrifying part of the whole experience was getting my IV put into my hand. Seeing anything go through skin scares the crap out of me, let alone having it go through my own skin. After that it was easy peasy walking into the operating room. I remember cheekily telling the surgeon not to rush—he came in a couple minutes late—and then I fell asleep.

When I woke up I knew where I was and what had happened. Boy, was I ever glad I went through with this. I felt no pain and took a picture of myself smiling to show Brett (my now boyfriend) that everything went well. My dad came in to see me and before I knew it we were walking out of the hospital with my new nose in its cast.

It was a really easy recovery, and if I had a job I would've been able to go back in a few days. What made me uncomfortable though was that I had to keep the cast on for a whole week and preferred not to be seen in public with it. I also had quite a bit of bruising under my eyes, looking like I had been in a huge fight. A couple days before my appointment to take off my cast I had taken it off on my own in my sleep. Even though my nose was extremely swollen, it still looked smaller than before surgery. Damn, this was phenomenal! I was pretty happy.

Every day there was improvement and the bruising went away pretty quickly. My new nose wasn't perfect, but it was a major improvement. I was so happy that I decided to get this done and this happiness only confirmed that I had made the right decision. Just because I went through the process so quickly doesn't mean I didn't give myself time to think it over. I had been wanting this for years. Once I knew it was the right time, I went for it. It's definitely not the answer for everyone, but for me, it has greatly increased my confidence. I don't think this would hold true if I had done it while I was depressed or extremely socially anxious.

I have no plans to get any other kind of plastic surgery done. After my rhinoplasty there was no part of me that thought other parts of my body needed fixing. I was beautiful the way I was.

Before and after my surgery I had been looking for a job, but was only able to get a couple interviews that led to rejection. I don't blame them, I hadn't had a job in four years. I was determined to find work that summer though, so I began to look into volunteer opportunities.

I found a volunteer position through my online search-
es that looked promising—an assistant counsellor at a
nonprofit organization's summer camp. I went through
the interview process and was picked as one of several vol-
unteers. That summer was such a rewarding experience,
working with children up to eighteen years old. They
taught me a lot and I hope that they got something out of
it from me being there too.

The last day of camp everyone was to write something
kind on a sticky note about each person. While all the
notes I got were incredibly kind, there was one that really
stood out to me: You're really quiet but when you do
talk you always have nice things to say. That helped
me to see that being quiet doesn't have to be a bad thing.
I'm always self-conscious about how quiet I am, which
makes me even quieter, but people do recognize that it's
just part of my personality. That even though I'm quiet,
I'm kind. I fear that sometimes my quietness comes off as
rude, but this camper showed me that he could see my
kindness. If he can see it, then I know others can too.

Returning to school in September, I decided to play a
much larger role in Active Minds. I attended every club
meeting and even ran one or two. I assisted during Brock's
residence move-in day as the only member (besides the
club executives, one of them being Brett). I tabled up to
twelve hours a week, which was more than all the execu-

tives except Brett. I spent hours preparing for tabling too, writing jokes and compliments to hand out to students. I decided that I wanted to increase the club's online presence, so I created an entire website, a YouTube channel, videos to raise mental health and suicide awareness, a brand-new logo for the club, and other graphics. What can I say, I'm a creative person.

I was so involved that some of the executives thought I was also an executive, and I'd have to remind them I wasn't. I was determined to be one next year. I hadn't applied for a position the previous year because elections were held less than a month after my first meeting. Plus, I didn't realize one of the positions even existed. I was committed to do everything I could to better the Active Minds club in every way I could despite not having a formal leadership position.

That December I was asked to help out with bringing a CAMH event to Brock called "One Brave Night." It's an overnight event in the spring for Canadians to raise money for mental health. I worked with staff from CAMH and Brock to bring the whole thing together with the help of some sponsors. I was directly involved in coming up with ideas of what to do, creating the itinerary, gaining a sponsor, marketing and more.

It felt so unbelievable to be making a difference with this event and with my part in Active Minds. This is what I wanted to do. Not necessarily planning events, but working for, or helping, a mental health nonprofit organization. Making a difference, increasing awareness, and putting my passion to use.

Everything I was working on for mental health made me happy. How had I not been involved in any extracurriculars throughout my first four years of university? This had become such a huge part of my life.

Once spring arrived, my role with mental health awareness was increasing. I applied for and was voted in as the Vice President of Active Minds for the next school year, with Brett taking the role of President. We had previously talked about this, deciding that he was a better fit for President because he was so vocal, while I was happier as more of a behind-the-scenes person. We were so excited, but the excitement didn't stop there. One Brave Night was a huge success, with me co-hosting, and it had such great feedback from students.

I was then asked to be one of four panelists to speak at an event regarding youth mental health. On the panel, I represented youth with lived experience, and the others were professionals in the field. That wasn't intimidating at all. The audience would be comprised of mostly parents and professionals, so I had to make sure my speech was up to par. I accepted the offer right away, preparing a ten-minute memorized speech that could knock people's socks off.

The day of my speech I had major diarrhea. This was a common occurrence for me but was more present than normal that day. I was so sick to my stomach and afraid I would keep going to the bathroom when I got to the event location. Thankfully I didn't have to go again, partially because there was nothing left in my stomach.

I was happy to have both my parents and Brett there, which ended up making my speech more impactful. How could I tell all these people about my experiences with depression and social anxiety without more emotion because my parents were there? I couldn't. And so that emotion carried into the audience.

As I got up on stage my fear went away and I just told my story. It was completely honest and it felt liberating. This was a much larger crowd than when I presented a speech with Active Minds' mental health event. I did get emotional knowing my family was there and when I got to the point where I told them that now I can look in the mirror and say "damn, I look good" instead of "I'm disgusting," they all cheered. When I finished the whole speech I got a huge round of applause and was told I did a fantastic job. I had brought people to tears. That was one of the greatest feelings I have ever felt.

After the whole event was over, I had quite a few people walk up to me, congratulating me and asking for advice. I helped out parents who were concerned for their daughter, doing my best to give them concrete advice on what could help and what worked for me. I wasn't a professional, but I truly hope my words were able to help them in some way.

That night led to speaking at another event, this one to more than three hundred summer students. I was still extremely nervous but my bowels were a bit more in control that day. I didn't get as emotional during that speech, probably because my loved ones weren't there and it was the second time I'd given it. Either way, I hope it came across as strong and authentic as it did the first time.

You told your truth and did great. Have more faith in yourself.

Just because I was having success in sharing my experience with mental health did not mean that I was cured. There were still many aspects of my life that took continual adjustment. One of these was sleeping.

My antidepressants have given me very vivid nightmares. Even with the changes in medication throughout the years, these nightmares continue to frequently reach me at least once a week, usually more. The first one I remember when on depression medication was of a witch stabbing my toes with the sharp tip of an umbrella. I could feel each stab prick through my toes, as I watched the blood seep out.

Another involved a man drilling broccoli into my skull as I sat strapped in a chair forced to watch people being shot, dead bodies piling up in an empty pool in front of me. Remember, these are the norm for me now, though I don't think I'll ever get used to them. Hell, I have had dreams within dreams within dreams. That's not a typo, it's like *Inception*.

Some of the time I know I'm in a dream, hoping with all of me that I will wake up so I don't have to feel the pain of being shot or tortured. Anytime I'm hurt in a dream it feels so real. Unbearably real. Sometimes I wake up screaming for help, with Brett—often staying over—calming me down, comforting me, and letting me know it's not real. Other nights he'll wake me up because I'm shaking, curled into a ball. But to the people I have told about some of these dreams, I stand by what I always say; I'd much rather have nightmares in my sleep than live in a nightmare.

—ee—

One night while living at school I experienced a bit of a living nightmare. My housemates were often loud down-stairs, and my bedroom was right above the family room. I was living in a different house from the year before.

Most of my housemates had left one weekend when I heard music and voices coming from downstairs. I thought it was weird that my one housemate, Emma, was having a fairly loud get-together with friends when it was something she had never done before, but I just put on my headphones and watched a movie in the safety of my bedroom. I fell asleep with the music on downstairs, people still talking.

Suddenly I heard yelling and was jolted awake at three in the morning. I couldn't hear Emma's voice, but another voice sounded similar to a different housemate. He must be downstairs, right? One person screaming was a house-mate's girlfriend, I recognized her voice right away. The other voice yelling was…my neighbour? The shrieking kept escalating and I was now not sure if any of my house-mates were even in the house. How did these other people get in? There were at least four people downstairs.

The argument downstairs carried on for about twen-ty minutes as I continued to question whether or not I should call the police. I was terrified, sitting in my bed sweating, staring back and forth between my phone and the door. There could potentially be someone who lives here downstairs, because otherwise, I didn't know how those people could have gotten in. But even if there was a housemate home, this was a huge argument that sounded as though it could become physical.

I should really call the police but what if the fight-ing stops by the time they come? What if I have to go downstairs to talk to them in my pyjamas? Do I just walk down now and yell at everyone to go home? Would I get punched? They were drinking, though…I wouldn't want anyone driving home; but the neighbours could at least walk home.

I kept struggling with a decision, listening to them yell about catching herpes. The yelling eventually died down and the girlfriend kicked out the neighbours, leaving only a couple people left in the house. I guess I just leave things the way they are?

I eventually fell asleep with my bedroom door locked, worried about what would happen in the morning. By the time I was up the girls had left. Holy crap, they technically broke into my house and I didn't call the police. Why was I so afraid to do so? Well, if a deadly peanut attack wasn't a good enough reason to call 911, then a break-in of teenagers wasn't important enough, right? I know it would have been best to call the police. Believe me, I know. If anyone ever breaks into a house I'm living in again I will call. I promise.

———ℓℓ⁓

I was able to get an internship at the head office of a financial institution that summer, after not working for five years. My extracurriculars were paying off more than I could have hoped. I could show on my resume that even though there was a gap in my experiences, I had been active recently in the community. During my phone interview, the interviewer told me he could hear the passion in my voice when I talked about Active Minds and the children at summer camp. I'm glad it showed through, because it was genuine.

The job itself was difficult but rewarding, giving me the feeling that my efforts were valued and truly making a difference. I worked as part of a team, all of us having to finish a certain number of files each month. I talked to team members about the job and often asked questions for clarification, but had difficulties with casual conversations. Although I had told myself I would do my best to be more outgoing at work, I still mostly stuck to myself. This is something I continue to try to improve.

CHAPTER NINE

BOUNCING BACK FROM FALLS

MOVING INTO A different apartment that September with new housemates, I was determined to be more outgoing. Not to the point of not being true to myself, but outgoing in the way I am with close friends and family. I was able to be more extroverted at first, but soon found myself getting comfortable doing homework in my room instead of in the main area. I still talked to my housemates, but not nearly as frequently as I would have liked. It was absolutely more than I had during the last two years of living with other people, so I would still call it a success.

Throughout the first couple weeks of classes I had some days where I felt discouraged and depressed. It was my final year of university, I had a part-time job during the school year with a mental health organization, the Paul Hansell Foundation, and I was the Vice President of Active Minds.

Although this excited me, I also felt enormous pressure. I needed to put my best effort into all three things: my schooling, my work, and my extracurriculars. This left me with less time to spend with Brett and my new housemates, but I knew I could figure out how to make everything work—other than on the days I doubted myself and felt slightly depressed. I pulled myself out of my funk by drinking tea, getting enough sleep, talking to Brett, and writing everything down I had to do—an idea I got from Brett while talking to him.

To better help my mental health and get me physically fit, I joined a Zumba class at school. The first week I missed because I was afraid of going. The next week I was depressed on that day. I was empty. Numb. Blank. This was different from anything I had experienced in a while. Not since my early years of university. Brett was with me that day and I was freaking him out; he had never seen me like this before. Everything I did was slow, my voice monotone, my eyes devoid of any emotions.

I'm going to have to quit school. Quit everything. I'm a failure. I've come all this way just to get depressed again and lose everything. What am I going to do with my life now? How pathetic of me to not even be able to take part in a dance class because I'm too scared.

I'd have the urge to cry, my eyes glassy, but then my eyes and mind would go empty again. I still wanted to try going to Zumba class, even though I knew I wouldn't make it through the doors.

As we sat on the bus to school, I stared into space the whole way. I felt as depressed as I used to during my bad days, minus the suicidal thoughts. We got off the bus, entered the school, and made it near the door to the dance class. I was barely talking to Brett on the whole way. I couldn't go in. Not only was I afraid of entering the class because of my social anxiety, but I physically was not capable of moving enough to dance. I didn't have the energy and every part of me refused to move more than was necessary.

Brett walked me outside and I burst out crying. I leaned on him for who knows how long, letting out all my emotions. This managed to make me feel slightly better, enough to be able to make it to his apartment. I still felt pretty empty, but now I didn't feel as if I'd never come out of that numb state.

The next day I felt normal again, no longer numb, and disturbed that I had gotten so depressed. Getting a full night's sleep cleared my mind, and I knew I would have to monitor my thoughts. After that day I didn't experience any more depressed days, except during PMS. I never did go to the Zumba class though, embarrassed that I had already missed the first couple weeks. I was doing well in my classes thankfully, excelling at my job and in Active Minds.

While I had made it through a hump of mental health difficulties, Brett was having his own. He decided it was best for him to take a break from school to better his mental health. I became the new president of Active Minds and maintained my responsibilities as vice president as well.

—ee—

Brett still came to visit me often, but sometimes he had to deal with my emotional bouts of PMS. He was pretty good with it, usually knowing what to say, but not always. Once we were watching an episode of *The 100*. A character I liked had been killed and I could not hold in my tears. By the end of the episode I was sobbing as if someone I knew had died.

Bear in mind that I often weep from movies and even some TV shows. I cried while watching *Lilo & Stitch*. So to me, it was no surprise that I was emotional. But when Brett tried to calm me down, he said the wrong words. He made a joke about turtles being used as hockey pucks to make me laugh. I don't know what made him think I'd laugh from that, and he immediately saw in my face that he had made a mistake. My sobbing got harder, tears soaking through his shirt.

"What if people actually play hockey with turtles as a puck?" I blubbered.

Brett told me no one ever would, but he couldn't prove it. I was sure there must have been someone at some time playing hockey with a turtle, upside down on its shell, spinning and sliding in fear. I couldn't handle that reality and so Brett did his best to calm me down. As he says, he was the "Sydney Crosby of boyfriend conversations" by being able to talk me down after his misstep. I remind him he wouldn't have had to talk me down from that if he hadn't made that awful joke in the first place. Now he knows never to joke about animals in any negative way or I'll basically fall apart.

Through my animal studies classes I've learned so much about the ways in which animals are exploited and the conditions they live in, that I have a difficult time seeing, hearing or reading anything graphic about animals. I felt the same way before my studies, don't get me wrong, but now I know so much more about the atrocities they go through, and it hurts me emotionally even more.

While scrolling through Facebook one night a video began playing automatically. It was of a piglet shaking on a metal grate, looking as if it were extremely sick or dying. I paused the video as quickly as I could and scrolled away, only having seen a few seconds, but that baby pig was etched into my brain. I burst out crying at the cruelties of the world, weeping for the piglet. No one deserves that. Controlling my tears was not an option so I had to miss a class. I felt slightly depressed the rest of that night, unable to take the image away from my mind as I fell asleep with tears running down my cheek.

—ℓ

I began my second semester missing the first week of classes. The day before heading back to school I was at a restaurant for a family gathering and was pulling up my pants in the washroom when I strained a muscle in my lower back. I felt a jolt of pain run from my back and down my thigh, almost causing me to fall, but the confined space of the stall kept me upright. I couldn't move at first, didn't have my phone on me, and was worried I could be stuck in there for a while. At least my extended family was fairly large; hopefully someone was drinking lots and would have to go to the washroom soon.

I attempted to put a bit of weight down on my right side, but couldn't do it. Trying again, I was able to do a little shuffle to move out of the stall. The pain was so intense that I had to hold back tears, but knew I needed to sit down somewhere. I waited a few minutes then slowly and stiffly limped out of the bathroom and back to my seat in the restaurant, awkwardly falling into my chair, unable to bend properly.

The next day I was still in a great deal of discomfort and saw a doctor for pain medication. I spent that first week of school sleeping almost all day and night, drowsy because of the medication.

I was able to go to school the second week, but by the third week I had somehow sprained my foot. I think it was from limping too much. Now I had pain not only in my back that wasn't fully recovered, but also my foot. I couldn't go to classes again as I had no crutches and could barely walk to my kitchen. It took months for that foot to finally heal completely, but in the meantime I had injured my other foot.

—⁣ℓ⁣—

Being just five minutes late to a class one night was enough to make me nervous, but I walked in anyway, only to find that nearly every seat was taken. The only openings I could see were in the front row, so I walked down the stairs to the front of the lecture hall of over a hundred students. When I got to the bottom there was a platform I had to step over to get to a seat, but as I crossed the platform I tripped and fell inelegantly on my hands and knees in front of a chair, bringing the lecture to a halt.

My adrenaline was rushing. The professor stepped off the stage to see if I was alright because I hadn't gotten back up right away. My one foot was twisted awkwardly underneath me and I had a feeling it was broken or sprained. I moved my foot carefully and there wasn't any pain, so I told her I was fine and took my seat.

As the adrenaline wore off though, the pain was immense. I could no longer move my foot at all and I was still feeling the embarrassment from falling. I held in my tears as I sat in the lecture for an hour, but once the break came my professor asked if I was okay. I broke out in tears and began hyperventilating, unable to control myself. This wasn't happening. Oh, please, no, this can't be hap-

pening. But it is. I desperately wanted to leave, but the
only way out was up the stairs and I was afraid of putting
any pressure on my foot. There was no way I could walk
on my own through the school to a bus or cab to get to
the hospital.

As I failed to control my crying and hyperventilating,
my professor called campus security to check out my foot
and take me to an ambulance. She also got me a bottle of
water to help calm me down. My freak out had subsided
by the time security arrived and I hobbled up the stairs
with their help, able to put a small amount of pressure on
my injured foot even though it was extremely painful.

We called 911 to ask for an ambulance and I thought I
would have to have help walking to where it was parked,
but they instead brought in a stretcher. I made my way
onto the stretcher as they strapped me in, a small crowd of
people watching. The paramedics rolled me through the
long hallways and I kept my head down, unable to face
the fact that everyone would be staring at me.

Once in the ambulance the paramedic who stayed with
me in the back checked my heart rate and said it was really fast. I told her I had social anxiety so what had just
happened really triggered me, but I undeniably felt calmer
in the ambulance away from so many eyes. A lot calmer.
Geez, I wonder what my heart rate was at before when I
was actually feeling exceptionally anxious?

After arriving at the hospital, getting registered, and
having x-rays done, I was told I had only sprained my
foot. I was given crutches but was still allowed to put some

pressure on that foot. Since crutches are death traps and I now knew I wasn't injuring myself more by putting weight on my foot, I used the crutches sparingly for a day.

The next time I had to go out I went sans crutches and did a tortoise walk. To me, that was less embarrassing than falling on my face with crutches flying in different directions. While stepping off the bus at school I put too much pressure on my newly sprained foot, and felt something within my ankle and foot shift. I almost fell over because the pain was excruciating and lasted about ten minutes, but then my foot felt much better. Almost healed. It seemed to me, and others I talked to, that something had dislocated when I originally fell.

Although the physical pain of that fall was gone, the emotional pain was still there. I was terrified of going to the lecture where I had embarrassed myself so I skipped it the next week. I also missed my seminar for that class.

I knew I had to go to lecture to pass the course so I forced myself to go, but was still too afraid of attending the seminar. At least in lecture I could sort of blend in. With the seminar, there were very few people and everyone would see me. I ended up not going to any more of the seminars for that course and it made me feel as if I was regressing.

Stop thinking that. Sometimes you have to move back first to get farther ahead. You're still pushing through. Just remember that your best is good enough. And I know you're giving it your all.

We were all required to do group presentations in front of the class in that course. I needed to do it to pass, and I couldn't let my group members down. Not everyone in the group had to talk in front of the class, but I volunteered to do some of the speaking. In fact, I had the largest part.

I was awfully nervous the night of our presentation, which was normal for me, but in this case I would have to face all of the people who saw me crumble. My group and I stepped onto the stage and I put on my happy face, pretending to have confidence. It worked. My voice did not shake, though my body did a bit but others probably didn't notice. I didn't mess up and I certainly didn't fall, all of us proud of how the whole presentation had went. Although I still did not go to seminars after that presentation, I knew that I had been successful in other ways.

During all of this I was still the President of Active Minds. In addition to Brett leaving, two other club executives had decided to take a leave of absence from school and so it was just me and one other girl with a smaller role. Mind you, one exec who left did still help out at some events so that made things easier. I had not only taken over as President but was acting as Vice President and Community Outreach (social media) all at once. Members were willing to step up and help out where they could, easing some of my anxiety.

Even though this was a lot to take on, I didn't get too overwhelmed. I was terrified of what could happen if it became too much to handle, but I did my best to remain calm and put my all into what I could. We still held events, we still held weekly meetings, and we still did almost everything that we used to do in previous years—plus more. I was still interning at the Paul Hansell Foundation and still helping out with bringing One Brave Night to Brock. And I had four classes.

This all would not have been possible if I wasn't in a healthy state of mind. Yes, some days it felt like too much and I would cry or go to sleep early, but I knew that the next day would be a reset. When I wake up in the morning I have a clear head, and sometimes that's all I need to do for my thoughts to be put in order.

One thing that was too much to take on was my finance course. The course that I had dropped out of years ago after breaking my foot. This time around I had to say enough is enough and take it online in the summer instead. The professor sped through lessons, had messy writing, and I had virtually no time for studying. On my midterm exam I got eighteen percent with no part marks anywhere and that was with just an hour of studying.

I knew that in order for me to do well in my other courses, job, and extracurriculars, dropping finance was the best decision. I'd graduate in October instead of June, but either way the end result would be the same. I'd finally graduate.

With one course less on my plate, my stress was reduced and I had more time to focus on other classes. This also gave me the chance to prepare for Active Minds events such as Speak Out Night which I was now organizing with staff and co-hosting, and One Brave Night for the second year in a row.

⁓

Another event I was quite looking forward to was the Clubs Awards Banquet for all Brock University clubs. Active Minds was nominated for five awards, including Most Improved Club, Club of the Year, Executive of the Year, and more. To be more specific, for the Executive of the Year award, I was nominated. Awesome, right? I was so excited that our club was nominated for awards. With all our hard work, I knew we deserved these nominations, but it would be even more remarkable if we won one of them. Or more.

The night of the banquet arrived and I went hand-in-hand with Brett for the third year in a row. I was a bundle of nerves. Although I had attended the previous two years as a member, we weren't nominated for many awards and certainly I never was. A couple other Active Minds members were there, the four of us a small group but full of energy. We grabbed some appetizers, chatted, and waited for the main event.

Soon the hosts got our attention and began going through some of the awards, drum rolls echoing across the room from our hands on the tables. Most Improved Club, not us. Several other awards, not us. Executive of the Year…Michelle Balge. Wait, what? My eyes watered, surprise and gratitude filling me. Holy crap, did I seriously just win? Whoa, this is amazing. Seriously amazing. They did say my name though, right? I wasn't imagining it?

Go on up, you deserve this.

After a few seconds of shock, and hugging Brett, I got up on stage, shaky as I was, to accept my award. I gave a quick speech and walked back to my table, struggling to hold back my emotions. I got a bunch of congratulations, even from people not in Active Minds, and I was so thankful. So, so thankful. We didn't end up winning any other awards that night, but what I did win meant so much to me. I had put my all into this club, for years, but even more so as an executive. It was great to see that others recognized this too.

———

Things were on the up and up. I really wanted to undertake tasks and I was just going for them. I registered for a finance course through an online university to take during the summer so I could still get my business minor. I was looking online at possible graduate programs I could attend related to either nonprofits or mental health, but kept coming back to programs for web design.

I have always had an interest in designing websites and have made several starting when I was about eleven or twelve. This and creating graphics were always a hobby of mine, but I never thought I could turn it into a career. Lo and behold, I found a great Web Design Graduate Certificate program at Sheridan College and decided to apply for it.

The next day I filled out an application, paid my fees, and sent in a portfolio. I was never this spontaneous in the past, but it was something I truly wanted so I thought, why the hell not? This way I can combine my different passions. I could design websites and graphics professionally, and do so for nonprofit organizations, particularly mental health and animal welfare organizations. Now that sounded like the ultimate dream job. To my surprise and excitement, I was accepted into the program the next month.

About a week after the spur of the moment decision to go to college, I decided to start writing a book. This book. It was something I've been wanting to do since the beginning of my recovery. In order to write the dark scenes I had to listen to Linkin Park on repeat. As soon as I was finished I'd turn off the music, wipe away my tears, and smile. Smiling for how far I have come in a few short years. Smiling at my accomplishments. Smiling at the fact that I didn't feel depressed when the music stopped. I felt good. I was me.

Although many parts of my life were going well, I still had setbacks. I did skip all but one seminar from the class where I sprained my foot in front of everyone. I also missed my very last class of university. I was not happy with myself.

—ee

Getting ready for my final class, excitement and nerves ran through me. I was excited to celebrate the end of university with classmates and we were all going to the campus bar after a short presentation so the professor could buy us each a beer. At the same time, this made me nervous. What if the few people I talked to aren't there? What if I'm awkward?

These nerves caused me to go to the bathroom for a while, making me late for my bus. Shit. I guess I'll just take the next bus and be a bit late. But what if I'm too late and by the time I get there they've already left the classroom to go to the bar?

My anxiety reached me down low again, and I returned to the bathroom. I got out with a couple of minutes to spare for me to barely catch the bus. But what if I'm late for the bus? I very well could be if the stop lights aren't working in my favour. Shit, now it's too late. There's no way I'll make the bus. Fuck, what is wrong with me? I've come so far just to miss my final class and even celebrate it with a free beer. Not cool. So not cool. I should've gone. I should've forced myself to go when I thought I may be late for the bus, but I didn't. Now I'm just lying here feeling sorry for myself.

Thoroughly disappointed, tears ran down my face. It would've been sublime to be able to tell people that I spent my final class of university at the bar with my professor, but now I could never say that. It was too late. Even more so, I had genuinely wanted to go. It was an engaging class with a professor that I loved, who took sincere interest in his students' success. I have had other professors and classes like this as well, but this was my final class. The one to remember. But I couldn't remember it because I never went.

I moped around for a few hours, wishing I could turn back time. But I can't. I have to keep going forward. Although missing that class is something I'd love to change, it's just not possible. So I'll do my best to work through things better in the future. Continuing to do my best is the most I can do, and the most I can do is good enough.

After my take-home exams were over—essentially just long essays done in the comfort of my own room—I moved back home, ready to begin my finance lessons online. My final course before I could graduate.

The first chapter I read caused me to get frustrated like when I originally took finance years ago. I kicked my feet on the couch and cried, worried this whole course would bring me down.

Remember, you aren't where you used to be. Talk it through with someone. You've got this.

I spoke to my mom and Brett, both of them able to help me put my thoughts together. This also prompted me to begin eating healthy and exercising again, which I had certainly slacked on for far too long.

The next day I tried again and had a bit of frustration but was able to make it through and on to other chapters. These first few chapters went well overall, then the difficult parts came. I was able to control my aggravation, but I didn't know if I would be able to finish the course in time.

Working on the first assignment, I had to look for help online for almost every question. When I saw what other people did to solve the problems it made complete sense to me, but it was how to know what formula to use in what question that confused me. Would I be able to finish this course in just two and a half months, including the exam? I didn't know.

I had a long talk with Brett. He was always able to help me clear my thoughts and get to what I really wanted. He helped me to see that I was afraid of being a failure. I was wanting this business minor more for myself than for my resume, so I could prove to myself that I wasn't inadequate. But the fact that I was putting all my effort into finance proved that I wasn't a failure. I was someone who perseveres. I just wasn't able to comprehend the material well enough in such a short amount of time. If I had more than two and a half months then I know I would be able to complete this course, but I had to finish it early so I could attend my web design program in September.

Withdrawing from finance was difficult, but it had to be done. It didn't mean I was a failure. Hell, this was my third time taking it. Not having a business minor doesn't mean that I suddenly just forgot everything else I learned from those courses. I still have that information and it can help me in the future.

What I wanted most was to take that web design program, so that's what I was going to focus on. Making sure my design skills were up to par so I could put my all into the program. I knew going to a new school in a completely different program than I was used to would be a test on my social anxiety, but I also knew that it would all be worth it. Totally worth it. Or so I hoped.

CHAPTER TEN

KEEP ON KEEPING ON

YES, IT WAS totally worth it. Or *is* totally worth it, since I'm still in school. During the first couple weeks of classes the professors would make jokes, asking if anyone regretted their decision so far to join the program. I could laugh along because, damn, am I ever glad I'm not regretting it. Not at all.

I'm thoroughly enjoying the content and look forward to going to school each day. We're a small program of twenty-two students, so I see the same people in every class.

This has thankfully made it easier to make friends with others, and it doesn't hurt that they're all approachable.

With superb classmates and professors, my social anxiety has been affecting me very little each day. Yes, I'm still shy and nervous, but to a normal extent. I feel comfortable in class most of the time and that's a brilliant feeling. I don't get fearful when told we're doing a group project. I don't get too anxious when presenting in front of the class. I'm just enjoying my time here. I still heat up when waiting in lines for food in the cafeteria, but that's something I've been working on. In time it will fade, and to get there I'm trying to reframe my thinking.

——ꝑ—

As I'm writing this at school, someone just asked to sit in the same booth as me to work on their laptop. My answer would always be yes, as it is today, but before my recovery I would've meant no.

After he sits down I'm feeling slightly on edge because I'm not talking to him, but most of me is okay with it. Would I rather be sitting alone? Yes. Would sitting alone have made me nervous in the past? Yes. Would sitting with him have made me nervous in the past? Hell yes. No way of winning back then.

Now, though, I was completely comfortable on my own and experiencing mild discomfort with a stranger sitting across from me. Not bad. I could start up a conversation, which is the part of me that feels nervous about being rude with my silence, but if he really wanted to talk to me I think he'd say something. I'm still not the best with social cues but I'm always trying to improve.

Hmm...I think I recognize him from a Facebook presentation I saw last night. If I ask if it's him, he may smile and say yes. If it's not the same person, he may get confused but say "no, it's not me." That's the worst that could happen. Though my body seems to think something way worse could happen because it's heating up. My muscles are tensing. I'm getting ready to ask him. I'm scared. But I'm going to test myself and ask him. Force myself. My heart's beating faster. Why am I doing this? I haven't talked to him for five minutes now, would it seem weird asking him a question now? Maybe, maybe not. Ok, here it goes. Shit, I'm scared. But let's do it. Deep breath. Okay, ask.

You can do this. One more deep breath, then ask. Prove to yourself that it's not so bad.

Okay, I'll ask. Even though my face is likely reddening right now. Oh god.

Just look up, and if it still looks like him, just ask. Everything's going to be alright.

I can do this. But, let's wait until he's done chewing.

"Umm, excuse me? I have a weird question, but did you do a Facebook presentation last night? I feel like it was you but I don't know."

"Nope, it wasn't me," he smiled at me, shaking his head.

Alright then, that was it. I did it. And it was the answer I was fearing, yet it was okay. I'm still overheated, yet thankfully not sweating, and my heart rate is slowing down. I did it. Now I'll stay sitting with him for another ten to fifteen minutes until I leave for a class. During those minutes sitting with him, my temperature and heart rate become normal again.

May I say that after that encounter I'm pretty darn proud of myself? Not only because I was able to ask him the question, but beyond that, I had no negative thoughts. None. I did ask myself if it would "seem weird" to ask him a question after five minutes of silence, but not that I, myself, was weird. If anything, I was encouraging. Rather than beat myself down, I built myself up. That is something to be proud of. And I don't need others' validation to feel proud of myself. So, ignore that "can I say I'm proud of myself?" question I asked before, because I can answer it myself, and it's a yes.

Looking back on the last several years, so many things have changed since I've improved my mental health. Beyond just school—which I can now go to with much ease—I've met up with Erin and Julia, my previous housemates, on separate occasions. We talked about the good times we had together and updated each other on where we are now in life.

I talk to them and one other housemate on Facebook occasionally, glad to know that we haven't lost touch. We're not nearly as close as we used to be, but how can we be as close as we were when we now live apart? No matter where we are in our lives I'll never forget our time spent together, the game nights, the movies, the baking, the loud neighbours upstairs who I swear were dropping bowling balls on the regular, or even the race to the bathrooms after a delicious but diarrhea-inducing dinner out. All of it.

My longtime friend Melissa and I chat more often and get together on occasion. I still find it so easy to talk to her when we catch up. We're currently in the same city which has made things easier, but reaching out to her more often is something I'd like to work on. The same goes for my other friends, like Kayla from high school. I want to continue to engage with them on Facebook and let them know that I am here, and I do care.

While I have yet to accomplish all the goals that I have set for myself, such as driving, I am at least open to the idea. The thought of it still scares me, but I do think that I'm ready to try on an empty road or parking lot. My fear is less: I can now go grocery shopping while pushing a cart, and walk outside whether I'm with my dog, Sophie, or not. Overall I just worry less about what others think of me and have less anxiety. This is still something I need to improve, but it's a difficult habit to kick. But I have been kicking it. In the nuts.

Now, here I am, ready to graduate from university while attending college. During my dark days, I didn't think either of those would ever be true. But they are. I've pushed myself farther than I thought possible, into the person I always wanted to be. I'll never be perfect—no one is—but I can be glad that I'm someone I'm happy with.

—⁄ℓ⁄—

It's the day of graduation and I'm a bundle of nerves. It's October, Friday the thirteenth, and the air is thick with moisture in the darkness of the morning. While this could easily make me fearful of bad luck, I somehow feel quite the opposite. Sure, I may trip while going up the stage, and no doubt that's part of why I'm nervous, but that's because I can be clumsy sometimes—or a lot of the time.

There's nothing in the air that's plotting against me, and I can choose whether or not to let an unlucky number or bad weather affect me. I choose to make it a positive. What are the odds that my graduation would fall on a day like today? Pretty low, and that makes it special to me. What were the odds, I used to think, that I could escape my depression and social anxiety? Pretty low, but I worked my way out and that's certainly special.

I'm going into today a bundle of nerves because that's just what happens to most people who must go on stage in front of who knows how many people. I'm feeling anxious and excited, both to be expected.

I have family and Brett going with me, all there to cheer me on. To congratulate me on my accomplishments, no matter how long they took. Eight years ago, I started university and thought my life was over. I wanted to die. I saw no future. My life meant nothing to me. But it meant something to others, and I trudged on. Am I ever glad that I kept going, finding the will to survive. Even if I didn't graduate, I'd be so proud of how far I've come, but being able to say that I made it through all that and still got a degree feels like a damn nice, juicy cherry on top of a fudge-filled sundae.

During our trip to the university, the seven of us barely fitting in the car, the sun came up and the moisture cleared. After dozing on and off from a lack of sleep, we made it to Brock with time to spare. We went our separate ways, me to get my gown and the others to their seats. I headed straight for a bathroom to cool and calm myself down, pumping myself up.

I know I can do this. I want to do this. It's going to be great. It's okay that I'm nervous, most people are in the same boat. It means I'm human. And sweating, that makes me human too. Just one that glistens more than others.

In the bathroom, I saw a girl I had known for a couple years and we congratulated each other, not realizing we were graduating at the same time. In fact, I'd see a few other people that day that I had gotten to know throughout my time at Brock. I may not have been as close friends with them as I would have liked to be, but they always put a smile on my face and I felt quite comfortable around them.

Nearly an hour later—we were off to a late start—all of us graduates walked uniformly into the large gym which held our convocation. I saw my loved ones as I walked down the aisle, my smile reflecting theirs. It's so surreal being here. I hadn't expected to feel so proud. Am I ever glad I could come to my graduation since I have Fridays off at college. This is something I'd never want to have missed.

Words of congratulations and encouragement were spoken to us by those on stage, letting us know how great of an accomplishment this was. A member of the Board of Trustees soon stepped up to the podium, handing out the Spirit of Brock medal for the one undergraduate student who best exemplified the spirit of Sir Isaac Brock through their courage, inspiration, leadership, innovation, and community involvement. I was then called to the stage to receive the award. Of all the students in the school, only one undergraduate and one graduate student received this award at graduation in the fall. And I was one of those people.

I was terrified and ecstatic, knowing I had to get up there to accept the award. My legs and hands shook as I walked toward the stage, the room roaring in applause. I shook the presenter's hand and he put the award around my neck, congratulating me.

The smile on my face couldn't be contained. The weight of that medal felt like I had accomplished the impossible.

Not that it was impossible to get to where I was, I mean, I am here, but there were many moments of defeat along the way. But it was the moments that I got back up that brought me here. Here, to a place where I'm being rewarded for fighting through my depression and social anxiety. Where the Board of Trustees acknowledges the difficulties of mental illness and recognizes the effort put forth by a student to help others.

As my mind returns to the present moment, we turn for pictures and I step off the side of the stage. It's a long zigzag ramp I have to go down, the room in complete silence until I make it back to my seat. Yes, this is an awesome moment, but feel free to keep the ceremony going.

Oh, god that was amazing, and awkward, and so fantastically perfect at the same time. Students around my seat congratulated me, and I thanked them all. This would be a moment I'd remember for the rest of my life.

I can't lie though and say I was surprised at hearing my name called for the award, because two weeks beforehand I received an email from Brock saying I had won the medal. At that point in time I was utterly shocked. And crying tears of happiness. Holy shitballs. All my hard work was paying off, and this was another way of reminding myself of that. It's heartwarming to know that others recognize it too.

One last amazing part to get through: I'd be happier once I was done getting onstage and had my degree.

Since my last name starts with a B—thanks Dad—I was up soon enough shaking hands and accepting my degree, everything running smoothly. Now I couldn't be happier. I opened the folder I was given and saw my fancy degree, then took a deep breath and smiled. I had done it. After years of perseverance, I had done it.

CHAPTER ELEVEN

BEAUTY BEYOND THE PAIN

MY DEPRESSION AND social anxiety have in part made me the person who I am today. They have shaped me to be a person who fully appreciates life and is wiser from it. I've learned a great deal about myself, who I am and who I want to be. I want to help others; I want to help people who are struggling with their own mental illnesses and show them that there is a bright light at the end of the tunnel. I also want to help animals, knowing they, too, experience mental illnesses from being in captivity, such as depression and PTSD (post-traumatic stress disorder).

I wouldn't have this much of a passion to help others if it weren't for my own illnesses. I'm thankful for them. Though they brought me the worst moments of my life, I can now experience the best moments to a higher degree than I ever thought possible. It's as if all the tears I cried were there for a reason, slowly watering my mind to allow for something beautiful to grow in place of the pain.

Every day I am happy I'm here. There's nowhere else I'd want to be. The tears that fall down my face are different than they used to be. Now I get to experience the full range of emotions. Not only sadness, anger and fright, but hope, happiness, and excitement. I can allow myself to feel down if something makes me upset and know that it's only temporary. It doesn't last. What does last is the joy in my heart.

I love my family, love my boyfriend, love my friends, and most importantly, I love myself. To truly hate who you are, with every fibre of your being, and slowly find ways to love yourself is an incredible feeling. I smile when I look in the mirror. I can say "damn, I look good today" with no negative thoughts in the back of my head. I can honestly be happy with who I see staring back at me. And what I see is someone who is full of love for herself and others, full of happiness, and full of life.

I love myself.

I am worthy.

I am beautiful.

I am strong.

I am intelligent.

I am too many things, it would take forever for me to finish.

I am fucking awesome.

EPILOGUE

I REALIZE THAT this memoir is about me, me, me and how I'm insecure, but this is what these illnesses can do to you. They trap you in your head. They make you believe thoughts that aren't true. They warp your sense of self. They corrupt your very being. They can pull and twist your true self out of you, leaving behind an empty shell. Depression and anxiety's hold on you, like a tight vine constricting your breath and body, can sometimes be too much to take.

That's why it's so important to reach out to people, even if it seems impossible. Letting out your emotions, giving yourself that release, can make a world of a difference. Even if it doesn't help as much as you'd like, it's a step in the right direction. That person can assist you in finding better help. We're all in this world together whether it seems like it or not, and there are people who care for you.

Please know that if you or anyone else is contemplating suicide, it is not a sign of weakness or an act of selfishness. It's an inability to cope and a state of complete hopelessness. Always take suicidal thoughts seriously as you can save someone's life, and don't be afraid to ask a person if they're considering suicide. Over time my family learned to ask me, and I'd give them an honest answer. It never put the thought in my head and only served as a reminder that they love me.

—ee—

Today, I don't believe that I will ever die by suicide. Even during periods when I didn't have suicidal thoughts I still assumed that's how I would die. But I have the tools to help me cope now, including people to talk to. I'm no longer hiding. I no longer want to hide. I am so proud of myself for coming this far, and I have gotten praise from loved ones. No matter what obstacles I face in the future I can handle them. I may not handle them all well, but I will make it through. Not everything will be easy moving forward and I may have setbacks, but that's okay. If I fall,

I will get back up. Even if it takes a couple of tries. Or many tries.

Social anxiety is something I will continue to fight, but that's just it. I'm fighting. Sometimes it gets the best of me, but I endlessly persevere. It does affect things that I do and say but each day I work on improving this. Although there are some situations in which I feel my illness has control, I refuse to allow it to have the hold on me that it once did. I'm still awkward as ever in social situations, but that's part of my charm. Or so I've been told.

For everyone reading this, I thank you. If you're facing your own challenges with mental illness, know that recovery is possible. Everyone's experiences are different, but what we all have in common is the strength to get through, even if it doesn't feel like it at the moment. We can build resilience to help prevent relapses. These setbacks may still happen, but they do not reflect upon your self-worth. You are always worthy of love, from others and yourself. Allow yourself to take pride in your accomplishments and reflect on what you're grateful for. Experience life for its beauty.

You may not believe what I'm saying yet, but through various aids such as cognitive behavioural therapy I am able to believe it for myself. And for you. No one deserves to live a life of sadness or fear.

Take a moment to observe your thoughts and if they are tearing you down, these thoughts aren't true. Find the roots and work your way up, proving every negative thought wrong. We will never get rid of all our negative thinking as that's a natural part of life, but if your core beliefs are that you're worth it and good enough, it can give you such a different outlook on life.

I'm not a professional, just passionate about advocating for mental health. Here are a couple of lists of what helped me with depression and social anxiety. Though they work for me, they may not all work for you and that's okay. There are more options elsewhere. Everyone is different and it could take time to figure out what is best. If you go to www.michellebalge.com, you'll find a collection of websites that may assist you with some items on these lists.

What can help you with depression:
- *Healthy eating*
- *Exercise*
- *Cognitive behavioural therapy*
  - *Chart your experiences, emotions, thoughts, and challenge those thoughts*
- *Make lists of triggers, coping strategies and people to call*
- *Track your symptoms*
- *Sunlight (can use therapy light)*
- *Meditation and mindfulness*
- *Breathing techniques*
- *Self-care*
- *See a therapist*
- *Have a good support system*

- *Medication*
- *List accomplishments, things you're grateful for*
- *Get eight hours of sleep*
  - *And maintain a regular sleep schedule*

What can help you with social anxiety:
- *Healthy eating*
- *Exercise*
- *Cognitive behavioural therapy*
  - *Create hierarchy of fears, face them gradually and repeatedly*
  - *Chart your experiences, emotions, thoughts, and challenge those thoughts*
- *Meditation and mindfulness*
- *Breathing techniques*
- *Self-care*
- *See a therapist*
- *Group therapy*
- *Try volunteering or joining something that interests you where you can meet people*
- *Have a good support system*
- *Medication*
- *List accomplishments*
- *Get eight hours of sleep*
  - *And maintain a regular sleep schedule*

Just like my story is not over, yours isn't either. Start doing things that make you happy. Whether it's as simple as taking a shower or as invigorating as running a marathon—but still showering afterwards—you deserve it. What is something you've always dreamed of? Reach for it. Go live your life. Really live it. You deserve it.

Love always,
Michelle

MENTAL HEALTH RESOURCES

Please note that at the time of publication all links and numbers are working. This may change in the future. If you or anyone else needs immediate help, please call your emergency number.

Canada Suicide Prevention Service (nationwide):
- Call: *1-833-456-4566* *(24/7)*
- Text: *45645* *(5pm-1am ET)*
- Chat: *crisisservicescanada.ca* *(5pm-1am ET)*
- For Quebec residents, call *1-866-APPELLE* *(24/7)*

Kids Help Phone (Canada, nationwide):
- Call: *1-800-668-6868 (24/7)*
- Chat: *kidshelpphone.ca (hours vary)*

US National Suicide Prevention Lifeline (nationwide):
- Call: *1-800-273-TALK (24/7)*
- Chat: *suicidepreventionlifeline.org (24/7)*

List of helplines across 16 countries (Australia, Belgium, Canada, China, England, France, India, Ireland, Japan, Netherlands, New Zealand, Scotland, Sri Lanka, United Kingdom, USA, Wales):
- *yourlifecounts.org/need-help/crisis-lines*

IMAlive online chat (global):
- *imalive.org (24/7)*

Suicide prevention:
- *suicideprevention.ca*
- *suicidology.org*

Understanding mental health and illness:
- *heretohelp.bc.ca*
- *cmha.ca/mental-health*
- *camh.ca/en/hospital/health_information*
- *helpguide.org*
- *beyondblue.org.au*

ACKNOWLEDGEMENTS

Thank you to everyone who helped make this book possible and supported me along the way. No words can describe how much I appreciate your efforts, but I'll try.

Mom and Dad, you've made me the person I am today. Thank you for all you've done and continue to do. Mom, thank you for letting me share a brief glimpse of your story.

Lindsay and Nicole, you're the best sisters anyone could ask for. Thank you for your continued love and support, and for allowing me to write a bit about you both. Nicole, thank you for reading through my book at the early stages and giving me feedback. Also, thank you for suffering through all my Facebook messages.

Grandma, you're such a strong woman and I really appreciate your willingness to share your experiences. Thank you for your love and support.

Brett, thank you for being there with me every step of the way. Your words of encouragement and love are always appreciated, and I love you with all my heart. Thank you for the fantastic idea of sharing lists of what has helped me with depression and social anxiety at the end of the book. Not only will it help others, but it's a great reminder for myself too.

Melissa, you're the best friend anyone could ask for. Thank you for always being there for me and reading through this memoir both before and after the editing stage. You were an early reader and a proof-reader, both invaluable. In addition to all of this, it was your idea to donate a portion of profits to a charity, and that will have a continued positive impact on CAMH.

Pam, you're also one of my best friends and have always been there for me. Thank you for being a proof-reader and supporter of not only this memoir, but me.

Cassandra, thank you for your amazing editing skills and kindness. You've been encouraging from the very beginning and this book would be incomplete without you.

Denise, Jill, and Marilyn, each of you brings a different point of view to mental health. Thank you for your excellent proof-reading and it's an honour to have you all a part of this book.

To all of those who had a hand in giving me feedback on the first cover (which I ended up not going with), thank you. This includes Christina, Melissa, Mariam, Nicole, Brett, and more. Although I didn't choose that cover, it means a lot to me that you were all willing to help.

Last but not least, Jenny. I contacted you several months before publication looking for a new cover design as I wasn't totally satisfied with what I came up with myself. The design you made for this book surpassed my expectations and I'm so proud to have it as the official cover.

ABOUT THE AUTHOR

If you've already read this book and aren't sneaking a peek at the back, you probably know a lot about me. Maybe more than you'd like to know. So here is a recap, plus a bit more.

Michelle Balge is a mental health advocate who has spoken about her mental health experiences at multiple events to students, the community, and professionals in the field. She was born and raised in Ontario, Canada, with a taste of city and small-town life.

Michelle graduated from Brock University with an Honours BA in Sociology and a Concentration in Critical Animal Studies. At graduation she was awarded with the Board of Trustees Spirit of Brock medal, given to the one undergraduate at fall convocation who best demonstrates the spirit of Sir Isaac Brock in leadership, courage, innovation, inspiration, and community involvement. While in university she was the president of a mental health club, Active Minds, for which she won the Executive of the Year award. Her biggest passions are mental health, animals, web design, helping the environment, and making a difference in these areas.

This year she will graduate from Sheridan College's Web Design Graduate Certificate program. For those of you reading this after June 2018, she's already graduated and probably had a blast at convocation. She is now (again, probably) flourishing in her web design career designing websites for nonprofit organizations, particularly in mental health and animal welfare.

You can find out more about Michelle and what she's actually doing at www.michellebalge.com.